LEGAL

The Gospel **According to** St. **Matt**hew

Warren Hicks

PULL (PAUSE || PRESS))

2020

Praise for This Book!

"Writing in the great traditions of Kurt Schwitters, William Burroughs and *Mad Magazine* (not to mention *Mad Libs*), Warren Hicks' *Begat* is an affectionate, irreverent, unapologetically juvenile, textual desacralization designed for maximum enjoyment."
— Amy White

"_____
_____
_____
_____
_____
_____"
— You

(Leave area blank for future praise.)

Less Flattering Praise

"This book is a crime scene. Every reader is a victim." – crooked cop

"If this book were any better, it'd almost be good enough to be considered bad. Almost."
– disgruntled rodeo clown

"Dude, what book were we talking about?"
– random stoner

"My cockatoo refused to poop on pages ripped from this stupid book. So, I did it for him. How's that for a blurb?" – former friend

"This book is better than the *Bible*! Don't quote me on that. Use this one instead: 'Satan has reared his ugly head, and he has a *wicked* sense of humor!' No. That still sounds too positive. Maybe…" – Pope Francis (*attributed*)

"Everyone should read this book, immediately! I don't want to be the only dumbass choking on regret for doing so." – mother-in-law

" [⚓ ⚓ ⚓] " – high school English teacher

"I loved the brilliant twist at the end, when everyone dies!" – some asshole that just spoiled the ending for everyone

If you can't convince someone staring at a blue square that it isn't a red circle, there's no point in wasting your time showing them a green triangle.

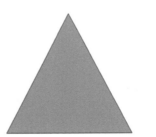

More time wasters by the author:

BegatBegatBegat.com
More of this nonsense. I'll probably have some prints available at some point. Might be worth your time, or not. Do whatever the hell you want. I'm not going to beg you. You already bought the book. Sucker!

WarrenHicks.com
Visual art: stuffed animal sculptures / photography / drawings / deadly baby rattles, etc.

e1ev1n.com
A conceptual self-portrait comprised of iPhone screen shots taken upon random observations of the times 1:11 and 11:11.

The Visual Arts Podcast
DontYouLieToMe.com
(producer)

Contact: BegatBegatBegat@gmail.com

BEGAT

****** WARNING *****

~~Hundreds of~~ ~~A few~~ *One* reader ~~complained~~ claims to have experienced ~~overwhelming joy,~~ vertigo and discombobulation while reading ~~every page~~ certain sections of this book. ~~Dozens have also~~ This *one* person, without any evidence, also ~~lied about~~ claimed to have heard ~~terrifying~~ voices in their head – pleasant ones at first. This is ~~not~~ normal. These voices will ~~never~~ eventually ~~trick~~ encourage you to ~~force~~ persuade your friends and family to ~~burn~~ buy this book, or else *many, many angels will die horrible deaths – one by one! Unicorns too!* If you begin to ~~fake~~ experience any of ~~this BS~~ these side effects, put the book down and slowly walk away. Dial 411. Ask for the number for 911. Calmly dial that number. You require psychiatric care. There is something seriously wrong with you. Have fun!

****

PULL (PAUSE || PRESS)

2020

Contact:
BegatBegatBegat@gmail.com

First Printing: August 2020

ISBN: 978-0-578-72778-3

Wow! I can't believe you're actually
reading this section. I never do. Not judging.
But, since you are reading this, I need a HUGE
favor. If you are a publisher or agent that might
be interested in this or future projects (who
wouldn't be, am I right?), please spread the
good word.

PULL 〔 PAUSE ||| PRESS ◖

(Not an actual publisher, yet.)

Cover and book design by Warren Hicks
Back cover photo courtesy of Jim Baumann

for Martha

honorable mentions:

Kurt Vonnegut, Jr.
Gary Larson (the Far Side)
Monty Python

Fun Quotes

"Religion is like a knife: you can either use it to cut bread or stick in someone's back."
— Desmond Tutu

"Anyone who thinks sitting in church can make you a Christian must also think that sitting in a garage can make you a car." — Garrison Keillor

"Religion is what keeps the poor from murdering the rich." — Napoleon Bonaparte

"The fact that a believer is happier than a skeptic is no more to the point than the fact that a drunken man is happier than a sober one."
— George Bernard Shaw

"I like your Christ. I do not like your Christians. Your Christians are so unlike your Christ."
— Mahatma Gandhi

"I'm completely in favor of the separation of Church and State. My idea is that these two institutions screw us up enough on their own, so both of them together is certain death."
— George Carlin

"It ain't the parts of the *Bible* that I can't understand that bother me, it's the parts that I do understand." — Mark Twain

"However many holy words you read, however many you speak, what good will they do you if you do not act on upon them?" – Buddha

"What if we picked the wrong religion? Every week, we're just making God madder and madder!" – Homer (Simpson)

"Religion is regarded by the common people as true, by the wise as false, and by the rulers as useful." – Seneca

"Give a man a fish, and you'll feed him for a day. Give him a religion, and he'll starve to death while praying for a fish." – Timothy Jones

"The problem with writing about religion is that you run the risk of offending sincerely religious people, and then they come after you with machetes." – Dave Barry

"All national institutions of churches, whether Jewish, Christian or [Islamic], appear to me no other than human inventions, set up to terrify and enslave mankind, and monopolize power and profit." – Thomas Paine

"When I was a kid I used to pray every night for a new bicycle. Then I realized that the Lord doesn't work that way. So I stole one and asked him to forgive me." – Emo Phillips

Half-assed illustrations by the author.

Contents

Boycott This Book!

Hurry! Be the first person on your block to be the last person, but not least, to sign the petition to boycott this heinous, extraordinarily bannable piece of garbage. That's right! *Your* signature will complete Phase 1 of the boycott.

Phase 2 is encouraging your friends and family to sign the petition as well. Ironically, each person needs to buy their own copy of *Begat* to gain access to the petition. Also, since the petition is on the last page, you need to read the entire book to get there. No page jumping! Sorry about that. LOL **#BoycottBegat**

Burn This Book!

NOTICE: All *Begat* sanctioned book-burning events in the U.S. have been postponed indefinitely due to the pandemic. (2020 can kiss my ass!) But you can join my email list at BegatBegatBegat.com for updates on future book-burning events in your area!

If you can't wait (why should you?), burn your copy in your own backyard – safely – then post images and videos on SM! **#BurnBegat**
Visit the above website to purchase more copies!

Acknowledgements

Without my amazing wife Martha, I would probably be mumbling myself to sleep while counting fingers in a corner of a padded cell instead of doing it in the comfort of our home. Without her encouragement and trust, this project would not have happened. Also, I am extremely fortunate to have an undeserved group of extremely gifted friends who volunteered as sounding boards and devil's advocates. Blame them if you don't like what you read. I will gladly provide their names and numbers.

Apologies

I am not apologizing for making this book. But I am sorry my family will more than likely be hurt because I did. This is not my intention. They will probably be horrified if they eventually catch wind of this (shh!) – god forbid they actually read it! I love them dearly and have struggled greatly with this knowledge throughout this project. I know their faith is what helps them survive this crazy world. It just doesn't work for me. Obviously.

Welcome!

Dear _____,
(Your Name Here)

Welcome to the head-bending, mind-scratching, ball-banging world of *Begat*, my extremely redacted edit of the Gospel of Matthew, from the New Testament of the Christian *Bible* – the King James Version – the one I was forced to read as a defenseless child.

********* **URGENT SIDEBAR** ********

1 – According to the *Bible*, true believers should *forgive* me if they find this book offensive, because that is what Jesus said they should do. (see page 157 under the heading: *Jesus Said WHAT!?*) I'm being serious! Read it!

2 – My beef isn't with genuine people of faith, just the hypocrites distorting the *Bible* to condemn everyone with opposing beliefs, or hiding criminal activity behind it. Fun examples: millionaire megachurch preachers, miracle healers, evangelists convicted of defrauding their congregants, politicking from the pulpit, self-righteous politicians, and a "God-anointed president" using the *Bible* as a political prop.

****

The *Bible* is edited every second of every day by those who decide which chapters, paragraphs, verses, or sentences to quote that endorse their preferred lifestyle, while blatantly ignoring the *multitude* that do not. By doing so, according to 80% of believers in the U.S., readers are, by definition, editing *the* word of God, or at the very least, words that were *inspired* by God.

Since self-editing the *Bible* for dubious reasons seems to be fair game for hypocrites, I decided to make my own personal edit of the Gospel of Matthew, with the sole purpose of making it as absurd as possible, and to better reflect *my* agenda: to make myself want to laugh like hell.

I know what you're probably thinking: "OMG! Am I going to hell if I continue reading?"

Great question! I'll make a bold prediction and say, yes. I mean, NO! Probably? Hell no! Only god knows. There is truly only one way to find out. Good luck!

Begat: According to Matt is more than just this awesome book. It is a multi-disciplinary body of work based on this book, which includes visual art, performance, animation, video, and music. Enjoy yourself! You've earned it!

******** **NON-URGENT SIDEBAR** ******

In case you are wondering, I'm not an atheist. Not that there is anything wrong with that. Some of my best friends are atheists. I even had an atheist for a roommate once. Once. If anything, I'm *closer* to agnostic. Personally, I believe there is some form of universal connectivity, but no one knows the answers, so why fight about it? (My god is better than your god! And he told me to kill you if you disagree. Sorry. Not sorry. Sucks to be you!)

At least in my warped mind, it seems a tad bit arrogant to believe we are the only form of "intelligent" life in such a vast universe filled with innumerable stars and planets. Besides, what makes humans so special? If you take a quick glance at our current state of affairs, humans really aren't that special at all. We are nothing but selfish meat sacks destroying everything we touch on this doomed planet, including each other. If we are some higher power's science project, I'd give them a failing grade. I'm really, really, not that impressed. I think another great flood is long overdue. On second thought, try something new, like crashing the moon into the Earth. Boom! That would have to be way more entertaining than watching humans and animals slowly drown.

****

Preface

In this section, I will be presenting highlights from my religious upbringing, including three self-proclaimed Christian merit badges to establish my credentials for writing this book. Pay attention. There will be a quiz. Focus, dammit!

I was incredibly lucky when I was brought into this world – albeit, without my permission. I was born into a loving, but mind-numbingly complicated Christian family that attends the Church of Christ, which is the correct and only denomination going to heaven. Whew! Baptists? Lutherans? Methodists? Nope! Sorry. Catholics? Oh, hell no! Don't get them started on Catholicism. My grandfather was a life-long Democrat, but he refused to vote for JFK because he was Catholic.

Despite my family's herculean efforts, I still do not believe the *Bible* is *the* word of God, or inspired by God, or that he even exists. But, out of respect, we avoid religious discussions. We agree that using faith or reason as an argument will not change our positions on the subject.

(Merit badge #1): My family dragged me to church three times a week: Sunday morning, Sunday night, and Wednesday night. I did that from birth until I turned eighteen. Put down your calculator. I've done the math for you: 3x52 weeks = 156 visits to church per year, minus 8

+/- for actual and successfully faked sick days. That brings us to approximately 148 services per year. 148x18 years = 2,664 +/- attendances in my lifetime. I really earned this badge!

Don't get me wrong, I had great times with my family and friends at church events. Our congregation was filled with caring, kind people that I love dearly. I don't judge anyone by their faith, but I do challenge them when they weaponize it to condemn others with opposing beliefs, and for political gain – which is exactly what the *Bible* says not to do.

Even as a kid I had questions, but only received questionable answers. Since my parents lied to me about Santa Claus and the Easter bunny, maybe they were lying to me about this egomaniacal old man with bipolar disorder (I am a jealous and vengeful god / I am a loving and forgiving god), who does nothing but sit in the clouds all day judging everyone.

And how uncool is it for him to command us to constantly thank him for creating us for the sole purpose of having us constantly thank him for creating us? He loves us, but if we don't thank him correctly, we'll burn in hell for an eternity. AND he keeps changing the rules, so it's really, really confusing. That doesn't sound like anyone I'd want to hang out with. Those are dickish moves!

The other two imaginary characters are much more likable by comparison. One is a creepy old man with a suspicious obsession with young children, and a raging elf fetish. It's ok though. He brings children gifts for not being bad. And he *doesn't* kill the ones who are. So, he's got that going for him, which is nice.

The other is a giant rabbit that poops out plastic eggs filled with candy and small treasures given to children, regardless of their disposition. So, obviously, all three characters are equally plausible.

The following actions are frowned upon by the church:

Good Libations: Okay. I'll accept over-indulgence as a valid concern. But when I asked why Jesus turned water into wine if we were not supposed to drink alcohol, their response: "Wine was non-alcoholic in those days." Say what? Then why didn't the *Bible* just say he turned water into grape juice? Or Kool-Aid? The latter makes more sense given billions have already drunk it.

Booty Shaking: Unquestionably sinful. Dancing provokes sexual thoughts. Don't blame dancing. Having genitals provokes sexual thoughts! And who gave us genitals? God? So, shouldn't we all be having as much sex as possible to please him? Let him know his handywork is appreciated. Don't be rude. Show some gratitude!

The Devil's Clothing: We were not allowed to wear shorts on church sanctioned trips. Sex!

Sex! Sex! No! No! No! Church camp was inhumane. July in Oklahoma is hotter than a metal bucket full of fried monkey balls wrapped in an electric blanket underneath a giant, angry hairdryer.

To ensure that no sexual thoughts were generated at camp, we had to wear jeans while playing sports in the blistering sun. Obviously, there was no swimming pool. Swimsuits? Oh, hell no! Chlorine can't wash away *those* sins.

When I was 12, I was kicked out of the car at the gate to this camp for the first time. All of my friends went to normal camps that had swimming pools, canoeing, basket welding, ritual orgies, etc. The good stuff. Anyway, blah, blah, blah. (Merit badge #2): I won the "Most Christ-like" award. Miracles do happen! Suck it, sinners!

Lucifer's Dream Box: This isn't related to our church, but I was baffled by a friend's house rules when I was seven or eight. He and his many siblings were not allowed to watch TV shows like *Bewitched*, *I Dream of Jeannie*, etc., because they contained "witchcraft." I kid you not. They were Baptists but I'm pretty sure this isn't part of their doctrine. So, I'm not sure where this was coming from. The Peace symbol was also prohibited because it was a broken, upside-down cross. Those rules always struck me as being kind of weird, even as a kid.

No! Hippies! Allowed!: My dad wouldn't let me grow my hair long as a teenager. I tried the, "But Jesus had long hair!" angle. He pointed out that it wasn't an actual photo of Jesus, just an artist's rendering, so there's no proof he had long hair. That only raised more questions about proof and faith. I had *faith* that Jesus did have long hair, but I needed *proof* that he actually existed.

(Merit badge #3): My baptismal certificate. I know what you're thinking: "Wait a minute! This awesome certificate says Tony, not Warren. This is a textbook example of fake news!"

Shut your word-hole! This isn't a textbook, yet. (Fingers crossed!) My middle name is Anthony. So, for some stupid reason my family called me Tony. Then one day I finally put my foot down and said, "No! I am not a Tony. My name is Warren, dammit!" True story.

In closing, if you weigh the gravity of all three merit badges combined, my qualifications for critiquing the *Bible* and getting really, really angry at hypocrites should be self-evident.

I do not profess to be faultless. I am guilty of a multitude of "sins." But at least I don't strip naked on national TV and twirl my dingle-dangle-doodle like a wet spaghetti noodle while forcefully condemning public nudity as a mortal sin. This probably isn't a textbook example of hypocrisy, but it should be.

Thanks for reading this far! I would have quit several pages ago. But wait, there's more! Keep reading! It might get better, or less worse.

Your pal,

_____
(Author's Signature)

Warren
_____
(Print Name)

Glossary

Yes, I know what you're thinking: "Hey, dumbass. The glossary belongs in the back of the book!"

Maybe. Maybe not. Maybe you should plug your word leak, bully! (I jest! You're my new BFF for reading this.) Why? Because I'm betting piles of counterfeit money that there are words and/or concepts that won't be familiar to you. I thought it would be more beneficial to provide the definitions ahead of the story, so you're *slightly* more prepared for what lies ahead. No extra charge. Your welcome!

Hopefully, this brave, bold, innovative move will enhance your reading experience. But, if this format is making you feel a little uneasy, please feel free to cut out this section and glue the pages to the back of the book. What do I care? You already paid for it.

Ape Horn: Sorry. There is no such thing. Or is there? I'm not giving away my intention. I guess you could call an erect ape penis a horn. Who am I to say that's an incorrect interpretation?

Bath Day: International day for finally taking a bath. Yes, some people need to be reminded. Once a year is better than never.

Borax: A sharp, heavy implement used for the permanent elimination of boring people at social gatherings. (Thanks to the pandemic it's currently rusting in a corner.)

Boron: A moron that's also incredibly boring. And being a moron doesn't protect you from the wrath of the borax. Is it still cool to say moron?

Cannibalism: Pretty much the only consistent theme happening throughout the book. And there's a lot of it! It would be weird if I was raised in a tribe of cannibals. I wouldn't have any say in the matter – just like I didn't have any say about being born a Christian. Who knows, people might taste delicious. Unless they're an asshole. Then I'll pass.

Cannabisism: A reasonable philosophy that teaches intaking THC in moderation is pretty dope.

Cannabist: A person that practices Cannabisism. Duh.

Cloathing: The things people wear to cover their bodies while they're loathing something, someone, or everything. Angry garments in general. See also: *haute hate*

Dream Urn™: A receptacle containing the ashes of your childhood dreams. Once it is filled, keep the Dream Urn™ prominently displayed on your office desk to remind you that it's your crappy job that forced you to set them on fire in the first place.

Dumb: a word created by someone that was dumb. What's up with the "b" on the end? If you say dum-buh, people are going to think you really are dum-buh. There isn't a "b" at the end of intelligence. It doesn't make any sense. Whyb notb haveb ab "b" atb theb endb ofb everyb wordb ifb it'sb suchb ab greatb ideab? English is dumb.

Eunuch: A dude, or an elf, post-castration. Sad.

Fire Water: A tasty adult beverage. But if you drink too much, you become vexed and a lunatic.

Fruit War: When people throw fruit at each other with the intent to maim or kill. It's quite wasteful, unless they're using rotten fruit. But soggy fruit won't do much damage, other than making your opponent smell bad.

Glory Cloth: Not to be confused with glory-hole.

Grinding: Google it.

Hand Tray: A severed human hand used as a tray, for cookies and what-not.

Hat Man: A man's hat that sprouted legs and eyes. Apparently, he has awkward social skills and easily offends others.

Land of Lace: It's basically a discounted version of Victoria's Secret.

Late Hen: Formerly known as an early bird. Late? Early? Doesn't really matter at this point. Time lost its meaning for her after her head was chopped off. Same thing probably happens to humans.

Liver Coven: A group of witches that were turned into statues made of liver. Their brooms and hats were pretty much left intact. Although one broom did get severely damaged. Purely accidental.

Mammon: I had to look this one up too. Hint: There is no such thing as a naked or woolly mammon.

Mighty Do: A badass haircut! Haters gonna hate.

Moon Tar: Basically, it's just tar dripping off the moon. But it did come from the moon. Hence: moon tar.

Moth: A flying bug that thinks a lightbulb is the moon. Not making fun. Just stating facts.

Moth Charger: An electrical cord designed for insertion into a moth's ass to provide warmth in the depths of winter. It can also cause a pleasant euphoria if left inserted long enough. But not too long.

Pair: Two pears. Actually, two of anything. The sentence, "Two pears", has a pair of words. I think that's how that works. Or do they have to be two of the same word – like, "Pear pear." That sentence doesn't make any sense, but it is a pair of pear words. Correct me if I'm wrong. I'm just winging it. Obviously, I could look it up and eliminate half of this unnecessarily long definition. But, since you've read this far, you're obviously smart enough to know what the word *pair* means. So, this rambling word sausage is probably an insult to you. My bad.

Pet House: A frat house for a wild variety of pets – from **A**sses to **Z**ebras! a/k/a the Poop Palace.

Pet Rock: A pet for lazy people. Stupendously lazy. People actually paid money for these!

Pipe: This is not a pipe.

Rad Elders: A small group of old, recovering hippies that actually bathe on at least a bi-weekly basis and have shunned the use of patchouli oil, drum circles, white-boy dreadlocks, and jam bands. They know they can't be completely forgiven for those heinous assaults on our senses, but they're pretty rad for even trying.

Thin House: Fairly self-explanatory.

Vest: The only garment I can think of that starts with a V. And DO NOT say V-neck sweater. It's still a sweater! Without the sweater, there's nothing but a V-neck, which is basically a crappy, cloth necklace, at best. Nice try.

Wedding Urn™: When you get divorced and burn every ounce of evidence that you were ever married to that asshole (gender neutral) and place the remains into a traditional urn. Eventually, you'll get tired of looking at it because it reminds you of the very evidence you tried to erase. So, now you dump the ashes into the litter box and destroy the newly emptied vessel with a hammer or nearest rock.

Yard Stew: The main ingredient is former ired laborers. Then add a couple of potatoes and season with local herbs – picked by pre-ired laborers.

Instructions

All references to religion have been redacted, except the devil and hell, which are universal human constructs. Biblical names, places, and events have also been redacted. No chapters, paragraphs, sentences, words, letters, or punctuation marks have been removed, added, or rearranged – only font treatments were used to define my edits.

Words in **bold, black font** matter. Words in ~~gray, strikethrough font~~ don't. Words in **bold, red font** are to be spoken aloud by the reader (you) during your reading experience, and by the audience during performances.

That's it! Now you can read. Huzzah!

{1:1} The book of the generation of Jesus Christ, the son of David, the son of Abraham. {1:2} Abraham begat Isaac; and Isaac begat Jacob; **a**nd Ja**cob** begat Judas and his brethren; {1:3} And Judas begat Phares and Zara of Thamar; and Phares begat Esrom; and Esrom

begat Aram; {1:4} And Aram begat Aminadab; and Aminadab begat Naasson; and Naasson begat Salmon; {1:5} And Salmon

begat Booz of Rachab**; and Booz begat** Obed of Ruth; and Obed begat Jesse; {1:6} And Jesse begat David **the king; and** David **the king begat** Solomon of her [that had been the wife] of Urias; {1:7} **And** Solomon **begat** Roboam; **and** Roboam **begat** Abia; and Abia **begat** Asa; {1:8} **And** Asa **begat** Josaphat; and Josaphat **begat** Joram; **and** Joram **begat** Ozias; {1:9} **And** Ozias **begat** Joatham; **and** Joatham **begat** Achaz; **and** Achaz **begat** Ezekias; {1:10} **And** Ezekias **begat** Manasses; **and** Manasses **begat** Amon; **and** Amon **begat** Josias; {1:11} **And** Josias **begat** Jechonias and his brethren, about the time they were carried away to Babylon:

11

[1:12] **And** after they were brought to Babylon, Jechonias **begat** Salathiel; **and** Salathiel **begat** Zorobabel; [1:13] **And** Zorobabel **begat** Abiud; **and** Abiud **begat** Eliakim; **and** Eliakim **begat** Azor; [1:14] **And** Azor **begat** Sadoc; **and** Sadoc **begat** Achim; **and** Achim **begat** Eliud; [1:15] **And** Eliud **begat** Eleazar; **and** Eleazar **begat** Matthan; **and** Matthan **begat** Jacob; [1:16] **And** Jacob **begat** Joseph the husband of Mary, of whom was born Jesus, who is called Christ. [1:17] So all the generations from Abraham to David [are] fourteen generations; and from David until the carrying away into **a** **Baby**lon [are] fourteen gene**rat**ions; and from the carrying away into Babylon unto Christ [are] fourteen generations**.**

[1:18] Now the birth of Jesus Christ **a** was on this **wise**: When as his **mother** Mary **was** espoused to Joseph, before they came together, she was **found with** child of **the** Holy **Ghost.** [BOO!] [1:19] Then Joseph **her husband,** being **a** just **man,** and not willing to make her a publick example, **was minded to put her away privily.** [1:20] **But** while he thought on these things**, behold,** the

12

angel of the Lord a**pear**ed unto him **in a dream, saying,** Joseph, thou son of David, **fear** not to take unto **thee** Mary **thy wife: for that which is conceived in her is** of the Holy **Ghost.** {1:21} **And she shall** bring forth a son, and thou shalt **call his name** JES**US:** **he shall** save his people from their sins. {1:22} Now all this was done, that it might be fulfilled which was s**poke**n of the Lord by the prophet, saying, {1:23} Behold, **a virgin** shall be with child, and shall bring forth a son, and they shall call his name Emmanuel, which being interpreted is, God with u**s**.

{1:24} Then Joseph being raised from sleep did as the angel of the Lord had bidden him, and took unto him his wife: {1:25} And knew her not till she had brought forth her firstborn son: and he **call**ed **his name** JES**US.**

{2:1} Now when Jes**us was born in** Bethlehem of Judaea in **the days of** Herod **the king,** behold, the**re** came **wise** men **from** the east to Jeru**salem**. {2:2} Say**ing, Where is** he that is born King of the Jews? for we have seen **his star** in the east, and are come to wor**ship** him. {2:3} When He**rod the king** had heard [these things,] he was troubled, and all Jerusalem with him. [2:4] And when he had **gathered all the** chief priests and scribes of the **people together,** he demanded of them where Christ should be born. [2:5] And they said unto him, In Bethlehem of Judaea: for thus it is writ**ten** by the prophet, [2:6] And thou Bethlehem, in the land of Juda, art not the least among the princes of Juda: for out of thee shall come a Governor, that shall rule my **people** Israel. [2:7] **Then** He**rod,** when he had privily **called the wise** men**, enquired of them** diligently **what time the star** appeared. [2:8] And he sent them to Bethlehem, and said, Go and search diligently for the young child; and when ye have found him, bring me word again,

that I may come and wor**ship** him also. [2:9] When they had heard the king, they **departed;** and, lo, the star, which they saw in the east, went before them, till **it** came and stood over where the young child **was** [2:10] **When they saw** the star, they rejoiced w**it**h exceeding great joy.

[2:11] And when **they** were **come into the house, they saw the young** child with Mary his moth**er, and** fell down, and worshipped him:

14

and when they had opened their treasures, they **presented** unto **him** gifts: gold and frank**incense**, and myrrh. {2:12} And being warned of God in a dream that they should not return to Herod, **they departed** into their own country another way.

{2:13} And when they were departed, **behold,** the angel of the Lord ap**pear**eth to Joseph **in a dream, saying,** Arise, and **take the young** child and his **moth**er, **and flee** into Egypt, and be thou there until I bring thee word: for Herod will seek the young child to **destroy** him. {2:14} When he arose, he took **the young** child and his **moth**er by night, and departed into Egypt: {2:15} And was there until the death of Herod: that it might be fulfilled which was spoken of the Lord by the prophet, saying, Out of Egypt have I called my son.

{2:16} **Then** He**rod,** when he **saw that he was** mocked of the **wise** men, was exceeding wroth, **and sent forth,** and slew **all the children** that were in Bethlehem, and in all the coasts thereof, **from two years old and under,** according **to**

15

the time which he had diligently enquired of the wise men. {2:17} Then was fulfilled that which was spoken by Jeremy the prophet, saying, {2:18} In Rama was there a voice heard, lamentation, and weeping, and **great** mourning, Rachel weeping [for] her **child**ren, and would not be com**fort**ed, because they are not.

{2:19} But when Herod was dead, **behold,** an angel of the Lord **a** **pear**eth **in a dream** to Joseph in Egypt, {2:20} **Saying,** Arise, and **take the young** child and his **moth**er, **and go into** the land of Israel: for they are dead which sought the young child's life. {2:21} And he arose, and took the young child and his mother, and came into the land of Israel. {2:22} But when he heard that Archelaus did reign in Judaea in **the room of** his **fat**her Herod, he was afraid to go thither: notwithstanding, **be**ing **warned of** God in **a dream**, he **turn**ed aside into the parts of Galilee: {2:23} And he came and dwelt in a city called Nazareth: that **it might be** ful**filled** which was spoken by the prophets, He shall be called a Nazarene.

reach **in the wilderness**
And say the king
is at **hand.** **Prepare**
his

camel's hair, and
his loins; his
meat was wild

, **and all**
round about **him**.

a **Sad**
rat
Bring
forth **fruits**

And think not to say
yourelves **have**
ham **you** **raise**
ham. **And now**

the axe is laid unto the root of the tree: therefore every tree which bringeth not forth good fruit is hewn down, and cast into the fire.

[3:11] I indeed baptize you with water unto repentance: but he that cometh after me is mightier than I, whose shoes I am not worthy to bear: he shall baptize you with the Holy Ghost, and [with] fire: [3:12] Whose fan [is] in his hand and he will throughly purge his floor, and gather his wheat into the garner: but he will burn up the chaff with unquenchable fire.

[3:13] Then cometh Jesus from Galilee to unto John, to be baptized of him. [3:14] But John forbad him, saying, I have need to be baptized of thee, and comest thou to me? [3:15] And Jesus answering said unto him, Suffer [it to be so] now: for thus it becometh us to fulfil all righteousness. Then he suffered him. [3:16] And Jesus, when he was baptized, went up straightway out of the water: and, lo, the heavens were opened unto him, and he saw the Spirit of God descending like a dove, and lighting upon him: [3:17] And lo a voice from

18

heaven, **saying,** This is my beloved Son, in whom **I am well** pleased.

{4:1} **Then** was Jesus **us led** up of the Spirit into **the wild**erness **to** be tempted of the devil. {4:2} And when he had **fast**ed forty **days and** forty **nights,** he was afterward an **hungred.** {4:3} And when the tempter came to him, **he said,** If thou be the Son of God, command that these stones be made bread. {4:4} But he answered and said, It is writ**ten,** Man shall not live by **bread** alone, but **by** every word that proceedeth out of the **mouth** of God. {4:5} **Then the devil taketh** him up into the holy city, and setteth him on a pinnacle of the temple. {4:6} And saith unto him, If thou be the Son of God, cast **thy self** down: for it is written**,** He shall give his angels charge concerning thee: **and** in [their] hands **the**y shall **bear** thee up, lest at any time thou dash thy foot against a stone**.**

{4:7} Jes**us said** unto him, It is written again, Thou shalt not tempt the Lord thy God. {4:8} Again, the devil taketh him up into an exceeding high mountain, and sheweth him all the kingdoms of the world, and the glory of them; {4:9} And saith unto him, All these **things will** I give thee, if thou wilt **fall down** and worship me. {4:10} **Then** saith Je **us** unto him, Get thee hence, **Sat**an: **for** it is written, **ten,** Thou shalt worship the Lord thy God, **and** him only shalt thou serve. {4:11} **Then** the devil **leaveth** him, and, behold, angels came and **mini**stered unto **him.**

{4:12} Now when Jes **us** had heard that John **was cast into prison, he departed** into Galilee; {4:13} And **leaving** Nazareth, he came **an**d dwelt in C **ape**rnaum, which is upon the sea coast, in the borders of Zabulon and Nephthalim: {4:14} That it might be **fulfilled** which was spoken by Esaias the prophet, saying, {4:15} The land of Zabulon, and the land of Nephthalim, [by] the way of the sea, beyond Jordan, Galilee of the Gentiles; {4:16} The people which sat in darkness saw great light; and to them which sat in the region and shadow of death light is sprung up. {4:17} From that time

us began to p**reach** **and** to **say,** Repent: for the king dom of heaven **is** at **hand.** [4:18]

And Je**us, walking by the sea** of Galilee**, saw** two brethren, Simon called Peter, and Andrew **his bro** ther, casting a net **in** to **the sea:** for they were fishers. [4:19] And **he saith** unto them, **Follow me**, and I will make you fishers of men. [4:20] **And** t**he** y straightway left [their] nets, and **followed** him. [4:21] And going on from thence, he saw other two brethren, James [the  son] of Zebedee, and John **his bro** ther, **in a ship** with Zebedee their father, mending their nets; and he called them. [4:22] **And** t**he** y **immediately left the ship** and their father, and followed him.

[4:23] And Jesus went about all Galilee, teaching in their synagogues, and preaching the gospel of **the king** dom, and healing all manner of sickness and all manner of disease among the people. [4:24] And his fame went throughout all Syria: and they **brought** unto him all sick **people** that were taken with divers diseases and torments, and those which were possessed with

devils, and those which were lunatick, and those that had the palsy; and he healed them. [4:25] **And** there followed him **great** multitudes of people from Galilee, and [from] De**cap**olis, and [from] Jeru**sale**m, and [from] Judaea, and [from] beyond Jordan**.**

[5:1] And seeing the multitudes, **he went up** into **a mountain: and** when he was set, his disciples came unto him: [5:2] And he **opened his mouth,** and taught them, **saying,** [5:3] Blessed [are] the poor in spirit: for **the**irs is the **king**dom of heaven. [5:4] Blessed [are] they that mourn: for they shall be comforted. [5:5] Blessed [are] the meek: for they **shall inherit** the earth. [5:6] B**less**ed [are] they which do hunger and thirst after righteousness: for they shall be filled. [5:7] Blessed [are] the merciful**:** for **he shall obtain** mercy. [5:8] B**less**ed [are] the pure in heart: for they shall see God**.**

{5:9} Blessed [are] the peacemakers: for they shall be **call**ed **the children** of God. {5:10} Blessed [are] **they** which are perse**cute**d for righteousness sake: for theirs is **the king**dom of heaven. {5:11} Blessed are ye, when [men] **shall revile you, and persecute [you,] and** shall **say all manner of evil against you** falsely, for my sake. {5:12} **Rejoice, and be exceeding glad**: for great [is] your reward in heaven: for so persecuted they theprophets which were before you.

{5:13} Ye are the **salt** of **the earth:** but if the salt have lost his savour, wherewith shall it be salted? **it is** thenceforth **good for nothing, but to be cast out, and** to be **trodden under foot** of men. {5:14} Ye are the light of  the world. A city that is set on an hill cannot be hid. {5:15} Neither do men light a candle, and put it under a bushel, but on a candlestick; and it giveth light unto all that are in the house. {5:16} **Let** your light so shine before **men**, that they may see your good works, and **glorify you**r Father which is in heaven.

23

{5:17} Think not that **I** am **come to destroy the** law, or the prophets: I am not come to destroy, but to fulfil. {5:18} For verily I say unto you, Till heaven and **earth** pass**,** one jot or **one tit**tle shall in no wise pass from the law, till all be fulfilled. {5:19} Whosoever therefore **shall break** one of these least commandments, and sh**all** teach **men** so, he shall be called the least in the kingdom of heaven: but whosoever shall do and teach [them,] the same shall be called great in the kingdom of heaven**.** {5:20} For I say unto you, That except your righteousness shall exceed [the righteousness] of the scribes and Pharisees, ye shall in no case enter into the kingdom of heaven.

{5:26} Verily **I say** unto thee**,** **Thou shalt by no means** come out thence, till thou hast paid the uttermost **fart**hing**.**

{5:27} Ye have heard that it was said by them of old time, Thou shalt not **commit adultery:** {5:28} But **I say unto you,** That whosoever looketh on a woman to lust after her hath **commit**ted **adultery with her already** in his heart**.** {5:29} **And if thy right eye offend thee,**

pluck it out, and cast [it] from thee: **for it is profitable** for thee that one of thy members should perish, and not [that] **thy whole body should be cast into hell.** {5:30} **And if thy right hand offend thee, cut it off,** and cast it from thee: **for it is profitable** for thee that one of thy members should perish, and not [that] **thy whole body should be cast into hell.** {5:31} It hath been said, Whosoever shall put away his wife, let him give her a writing of divorcement: {5:32} But I say unto you, That whosoever shall **put away his wife, saving for** the cause of **fornication,** causeth her to commit adultery: **and** whosoever shall marry her that is divorced committeth **adultery.**

{5:33} Again, ye have heard that it hath been said by them of old time, Thou shalt not for**swear** thyself, but shalt perform unto the Lord thine oaths: {5:34} But **I say unto you, Swear** not at all; neither by heaven; for it is God's throne: {5:35} Nor by the earth; for **it is his footstool:** neither by Jerusalem; for **it is** the city of the **great** King. {5:36} Neither shalt thou s**wear** by **thy** head, because thou canst not make one **hair white or**

25

black. [5:37] But let your communication be Yea, yea. Nay, nay: for whatsoever is more than these cometh of evil.

[5:38] Ye have heard that it hath been said, An eye for an eye, and a tooth for a tooth: [5:39] But I say unto you, That ye resist not evil: but whosoever shall smite thee on thy right cheek, turn to him the other also. [5:40] And if any man will sue thee at the law, and take away thy coat, let him have [thy] cloke also. [5:41] And whosoever shall compel thee to go a mile, go with him twain. [5:42] Give to him that asketh thee, and from him that would borrow the urn not thou away.

[5:43] Ye have heard that i hath been said, Thou shalt love thy neighbour, and hate thine enemy. [5:44] But I say unto you, Love your enemies, bless them that curse you, do good to them that hate you, and pray for them which despitefully use you, and persecute you; [5:45] That ye may be the children of your Father which is in heaven: for he maketh his sun to rise on the evil and on the good, and sendeth rain on he just and on the unjust. {5:46} **For i**f ye **love** them which **love** you, what reward have ye? do not even **the pub**licans the same? {5:47} And if ye **salute** your brethren only, what do ye more [than others?] do not even **the pub**licans so? {5:48} Be ye therefore perfect, even as your Father **which is** in heaven is **perfect. [DRINK]**

{6:1} **Take** heed that ye do not your alms before men, to be seen of them: otherwise ye have no reward of **your** Father which is in heaven. {6:2} Therefore when thou doest [thine] alms, do not sound a t**rum**pet before thee, as the hypocrites do in the synagogues and in the streets, that they may have glory of men. Verily I say un**to** you. They have their re**war**d. {6:3} But when thou doest alms, let not thy left hand know what thy right hand doeth: {6:4} That thine alms may be in secret: and thy **[WHISPER]** Fa**the**r which seeth in **secret** hims**elf** shall re**war**d thee openly.

{6:7} But when ye pray, **use** not **vain repetitions,** as **the heathen** [do:] for they think that they **shall be heard** for their much **speaking.** {6:8} Be not ye therefore like unto them: for your Father knoweth what things ye have need of, before ye ask him.

{6:9} After this manner therefore pray ye: Our Father which art in heaven, Hallowed be thy name. {6:10} Thy kingdom come. Thy will be done in earth, as [it is] in heaven. {6:11} **Give us** this day **our daily bread.** {6:12} And for**give us** our debts, as we forgive **our** debtors. {6:13} And lead us not into temptation, but deliver us from **evil.** For thine is the kingdom, and the **power,** and the glory, for ever. Amen.

{6:14} For if ye **forgive** men **their** tres**asses,** your heavenly Father will also forgive you: {6:15} **But** if ye **forgive not** men **their asses,** neither will your Father for**or**give **your** tresp**ass** .

{6:16} Moreover when ye fast, be not, as **the hypocrites** of a **sad** countenance: for they disfigure their **faces,** that they **may appear** unto men to fast. Verily I say unto you, **They have**

their reward. {6:17} But thou, when thou fastest, anoint thine head, and wash thy face; {6:18} That thou appear not unto men to fast, but unto thy Father which is **[WHISPER]** in secret: and thy Father, which seeth in secret, shall reward thee openly.

{6:19} Lay not up for your elves treasures upon earth, where moth and rust doth corrupt, and where thieves break through and steal: {6:20} But lay up for your elves treasures in heaven, where neither moth nor rust doth corrupt, and where thieves do not break through nor steal: {6:21} For where your treasure is, there will your heart be also. {6:22} The light of the body is the eye: if therefore thine eye be single, thy whole body shall be full of light. {6:23} But if thine eye be evil, thy whole body shall be full of darkness. If therefore the light that is in thee be darkness, how great [is] that darkness!

{6:24} No man can serve two masters: for either he will hate the one, and love the other; or else he will hold to the one, and despise the other. Ye cannot **serve** God and **mammon.** [6:25] Therefore **I say** unto **to you,** Take no thought for your life, what ye shall **eat or** what ye shall **drink** nor yet for **your body,** what ye shall put **on. Is not** the **life more** than **meat,** and

the body than raiment? [6:26] Behold the fowls of the air: for they sow not, neither do they reap, nor gather into barns: yet your heavenly Father feedeth them. Are ye not much better than they?

[6:27] **Which of you** by taking thought **can add** one cubit unto his stature**?** [6:28] And why take ye thought for raiment? **Consider** the lilies of the field, **how they** grow; they toil not, neither do they **spin:** [6:29] **And yet I say** unto you, That even Solomon **in** all **his glory** was not arrayed like one of these. [6:30] Wherefore, if God so

cloth the **grass** of the field, which to day is, and to morrow is cast into **the oven,** [shall he] not much **more** [**cloth**e you, O] ye of little faith**?** [6:31] Therefore take no thought, saying, What shall **we eat**? or, What shall **we drink**? or, **Where**withal shall we **be**

clothed? {6:32} (For after **all these things** do
the Gentiles **see**k:) for **your** heavenly Father
kneweth that ye have need of all these **things.**
{6:33} But seek ye first the kingdom of God, and

his righteousness: **and all these
things shall be added** unto you.
{6:34} Take **therefore** no
thought for the morrow: for the
morrow shall take thought for
the things of it**self.** Sufficient unto the day **is**
the **evil** thereof.

{7:1} **Judge** not, **that** ye be not **judge**d. {7:2}
For with what **judgment ye judge,** ye **shall be
judged:** and with what measure ye mete, it shall
be **measure**d to you again. {7:3} And why
beholdest thou the mote that is in **thy brother's
eye,** but considerest not the beam that is in thine
own eye? {7:4} Or how wilt thou **say to thy
bro**ther, **Let me pull out
the** mote out of thine
eye; and behold, a beam
is in **thine own eye?**

{7:5} **Thou hypocrite, first cast out** the beam
out of **thine own eye; and then** shalt thou see
clearly to **cast out** the mote out of **thy brother's
eye.**

31

[7:6] Give not that which is holy unto **the dogs** neither **cast ye** your **pearls** before swine; lest they trample them under **the** r feet, and turn **again** and rend you.

[7:7] Ask, and it shall be **give** n you; **seek,** ye shall **find; knock, and** it shall be **open** ed unto you: [7:8] For every one that **asketh receiveth;** and he that **seeketh findeth; and** to him that **knocketh it** shall be **open** ed. [7:9] Or what man is there of you, whom if his son ask bread, will he give him a stone?

[7:10] Or if he **ask a fish** will he give him a serpent **?** [7:11] If ye then, **be** ing **evil** , know how to give good gifts

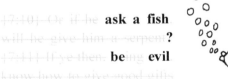

unto **to your children,** how much more shall your Father which is in heaven **give good things to them** that ask him? [7:12] Therefore all things whatsoever ye would that men should do to you **,** do ye even so to them: **for this is the law** and the prophets **.**

[7:13] **Enter** ye in at **the** strait **gate: for** wide [is] **the gate** , and broad [is] **the way** that leadeth

to destruction, and **many** there be which **go in there**: {7:14} **Because** strait **it is the gate,** and narrow **is the way, which leadeth** unto life, and few **there** be that find it.

{7:15} **Beware of** false prophets, which come to you in **sheep's** clothing **thing** but **in**wardly **the**y are **rave**ning wolves. {7:16} Ye shall know them by their fruits. **Do men gather** grapes **of** thorns, **horns,** or figs of thistles**?**

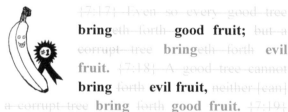

{7:17} Even so every good tree **bring**eth forth **good fruit;** but a corrupt tree **bring**eth forth **evil fruit.** {7:18} A good tree cannot **bring** forth **evil fruit,** neither can a corrupt tree **bring** forth **good fruit.** {7:19} Every tree that **bringeth not** forth

good fruit is hewn down**, and cast into the fire.** {7:20} Wherefore by **the**ir **fruit**s ye **shall know** them.

33

every one that saith unto me, Lord, Lord, shall enter into the kingdom of heaven; but he that doeth the will of my Father which is in heaven. {7:22} Many **will say** to me in that day, Lord, Lord, have we not prophesied in thy name? and **i**n thy name **am** have c**a**st out **devil**? and in thy name **do many wonder**ful works **?** {7:23} And then will **I profess** unto them, I **never** knew you: depart from me, ye that **work** iniquity.

{7:24} Therefore whosoever heareth these sayings of mine, and doeth them, I will liken him unto **a** wise **man**, which **built his house upon a rock:** {7:25} And the rain descended, and the

floods came, and the winds blew, and beat upon that house; and it fell not: for **it was found**ed **upon a rock.** {7:26} And every one that heareth these sayings of mine, and doeth them not, shall be likened unto **a fool**ish man, which built his house upon the sand: {7:27} And the rain descended, and the floods came, and the winds **blew**, and beat **up**on **that house; and it fell: and** great was the fall of it. {7:28} And it came to p**ass**, when Jesus had

ended these sayings. **the people** were astonished at his doctrine: {7:29} For he taught them as [one] having authority, and not as the scribes.

{8:1} When he was come down from the mountain, gr**eat multitudes** followed him. {8:2} And, behold, there came a leper and worshipped him, saying, Lord, if thou wilt, thou canst make me clean. {8:3} And Jesus put forth [his] hand, and touched him, saying, I

will, **be** thou **clean. And immediately** his leprosy was **clean**sed. {8:4} And Jesus saith unto him, See thou tell **no man**: **but** go thy way, shew **thy**self to the priest, and offer the gift that Moses commanded, for a testimony unto them.

{8:5} **An**d when Jesus was entered into C**ape**rnaum, there **came** unto him a centurion, beseeching him, {8:6} And **saying,** Lord, **my**

serv**ant lieth at home sick** of the palsy, **grievously tormented.** {8:7} And Jes**us saith** unto him, I will come and heal him. {8:8} The centurion answered and said,

Lord, I am not worthy that thou shouldest come **under my roof:** but speak the word only, and my servant shall be healed.

{8:9} **For I am a man** under authority, having soldiers under me: **and** I say to **this** man **Go, and** he **goeth; and** to another **Come, and** he **cometh;** and to my servant **Do this,** and he doeth **it.** {8:10} When Jesus **heard** it, **he** marvelled, and **said** to them that followed, Verily **I say** unto you, I have not found so great faith, no, not in Israel. {8:11} And **I say** unto you, That many shall come from **the east and west,** and **shall sit down with A**bra**ham, and** Isaac **a**nd Jacob **cob,** in the kingdom of heaven.

{8:12} But **the children** of the kingdom shall be cast out into outer darkness: there **shall** be weeping and gnashing of teeth. {8:13} And Jesus said unto the centurion, **Go** thy way; and as thou hast believed, so be it done un**to** thee. And his servant was healed in **the** self**elf**same hour.

{8:14} **And when** Jesus **us was** come in**in** to **Pet**er's **house,** he saw **his** wife's **moth**er **laid** and **sick of a fever.** {8:15} And he touched her hand, and the fever left her: and she arose and ministered unto them.

{8:16} When the even was come, **they brought** unto **him** many that were possessed with **devil**s: and he cast out the spirits with [his] word, and healed all that were sick: {8:17} That it might be fulfilled which was spoken by Esaias the prophet, saying, Hims**elf** took our in**firm**ities, **and bare** [our] sicknesses.

{8:18} Now when Jesus saw gr**eat multitudes** about him, he gave comm**and**ment to **depart** un**to the other side.** {8:19} And a certain scribe came, and said unto him, Master, I will follow thee whithersoever thou goest. {8:20} And Jes**us saith** unto him**, The foxes have holes, and the bird**s of the air [have] nests; but the Son of **man** hath not where to lay [h**is**] head. {8:21} And another of his disciples said unto him, Lord, suffer me first to go and bury my **fat**her.

{8:22} But Jesus said unto him, Follow me; and let the dead bury their dead. {8:23} And when he was entered into a ship, his disciples

followed him. {8:24} And **behold,** there arose
a great tem**pest in the sea,** insomuch that the
ship was covered with the waves: but he was
asleep. {8:25} And his disciples came to [him,]
and awoke him, **saying,** Lord, save us: we
perish. {8:26} And he saith unto them, **Why
are ye** fearful, O ye of little faith? Then he
arose, and rebuked the winds and the sea; and
there was a great **calm.** {8:27} But the men
marvelled, saying, What **man**ner of **man** is
this, that even the winds and the sea obey him**!**

{8:28} **And when he** was **come to the other
side** into the country of the Gergesenes, t**he**re
met him **two** possessed with **devils,** coming out
of the tombs, exceeding fierce, so that no man
might pass by that way. {8:29} **And** behold,
they cried out, saying, What have we to do
with thee, Jesus, thou Son of God? art thou come
hither **to torment** us **the time?** {8:30} And
there was a good way off from them an **herd of
many swine** feeding. {8:31} So **the devils**
besought him, **say**ing, If thou cast us out, **suffer**

38

us to go away into the herd of swine. {8:32} And he said unto them, Go. And when they were come out, they went into the herd of swine: **and**, behold, **the whole herd of swine ran violently down a steep place** into the sea, **and** perished in the waters. {8:33} And they that kept them fled, and went their ways **into the** city, and told every thing, and what was befallen to the possessed of the **devils.** {8:34} And, behold, the **w hole** city came out to meet Jesus: and when they saw him, they besought [him] that he would depart out of their coasts**.**

{9:1} And he entered into a ship, and passed over, and came into his own city. {9:2} And, **behold,** they brought to him **a man sick of** the palsy, **lying on a bed:** and Jesus seeing their faith **said** unto the sick of the palsy; Son, be of good cheer; thy sins be for**give**n thee. {9:3} And, behold, certain of the scribes said within **the**mselves, **This** [man] blasphe**meth.** {9:4} And Jesus **know**ing **their thoughts** said, Wherefore **think** ye **evil** in your hearts? {9:5}

give the sick pal thy bed, and go to thin house. he departed to his house.

us passed a man named sitting tom, And he followed him.

us eat in the pub and sat down they said, Why eat us said,

be whole I need not a physician, but they that are sick. {9:13} But go ye and learn what [that] meaneth, I will have mercy, and not sacrifice: for I am not come me to call the righteous, but sinners to repentance.

{9:14} Then he came to him the disciples of John, saying, Why do we and the Pharisees fast oft, but thy disciples fast not? {9:15} And Jesus us said unto them, Can the children of the bride ride chamber mourn, our as long as the bride ride groom is with them? but the days will come, when the bridegroom shall be taken from them, and then shall they fast.

{9:16} No man putteth a piece of new cloth unto an old garment, for that which is put in to fill it up taketh from the garment, and the rent is made worse.

{9:17} Neither do men put new wine into old bottles: else the bottles break, and the wine runneth out, and the bottles perish: but they put new wine into new bottles, and both are reserved.

behold, **dead** **woman** **with** **twelve years** **her elf [I]**

may **touch his garment** **us turned** **, he said,** **comfort** **the** **hole. And** **he** **made** **hole** **that hour.**

us **said** **,** **the**
maid is **dead** **they laughed** [LAUGH!]

And when us **departed**, **two blind men followed him**. **behold,** **a dumb man with a devil.** **And the devil was dumb** .

43

kingdom, and healing every sickness and every disease among the people.

[9:36] But when **he saw the multitudes** he was moved with comp**ass**ion on them**, because they fainted, and were scattered abroad, as sheep** having no shepherd. [9:37] Then saith he unto his disciples, **The** har**vest** truly **is** plenteous, but the labo**our**ers [are] few; [9:38] Pray ye therefore the Lord of the har**vest,** that he will **send forth** labo**our**ers into his har**vest.**

[10:1] And when **he had** called unto [him] his twelve disciples, he gave **them power** [against] un**clean** spirits, to cast them out, and to heal all manner of sickness and all manner of disease. [10:2] Now the names of the twelve apostles are these; The first, Simon, who is called Peter, and Andrew **his** brother; James [the son] of Ze**bed**ee, and John his brother; [10:3] Philip, and Bartholomew; Thomas, and Ma**at**thew **the** pub**lican**; James [the son] of

44

Alphaeus, and Lebbaeus, whose surname was Thaddaeus; {10:4} Simon the Canaanite, and Judas Iscariot, who also betrayed him**.**

{10:5} These twelve Jes**us sent** forth, and commanded **them,** **saying, Go** not **into the** way of the Gentiles, and into [any] city of the Samaritans enter ye not: {10:6} But go **rat**her to the lost sheep of the **house** of Israel. {10:7} **And** as ye go, p**reach, saying, The king**dom of heaven **is** a**t hand.** {10:8} Heal the sick, cleanse the lepers, raise the dead, cast out devils: freely ye have received, freely give.

{10:9} **Provide** neither **gold,** n**or silver,** n**or** **brass in your purses,** {10:10} Nor se**rip** for **[your]** journey, neither **two coats,** n**either** **shoe** , nor yet staves: f**or** the workman is **worthy** of his **meat.** {10:11} And into **what**so**ever** city or town ye shall enter, enquire who in it is worthy; and there abide till ye go thence.

{10:12} And when ye come into an house, **salute** it. {10:13} And if **the** house be worthy,

45

let your **ace** come upon it: but if it be not worthy**, let your** p**ace** return to you. [10:14] And whosoever shall not receive you, nor hear your words, when ye depart out of that house or city, shake off the **dust** of **your feet.** [10:15] Verily I say unto you, **It shall be more tolerable** for the land of  Sodom and Gomorrha in the day of judgment, than for that city.

[10:16] **Behold, I send you** forth **a sheep** in the midst of wolves: be ye therefore wise as serpents, and harmless as doves**. [10:17] But beware of** men: for **the**y will de**liver** you up to

 the councils, and they will scourge you in their synagogues; [10:18] And ye shall be brought before governors and kings for my sake, for a testimony against them **and** the Gentiles. [10:19] But when **the**y de**liver** you up, take no thought how or what ye **shall speak:** **for it shall be** given you in that same hour **what ye shall speak.** [10:20] **For it is** not **ye that speak,** but the Spirit of your Father **which speaketh in you.**

[10:21] And the brother shall deliver up the brother to death, and **the fat**her the child: and the **children shall rise up** against [their] parents, and cause them to be put to **eat**h. [10:22] **And ye shall** be **hate**d of all [**men**] for my name's sake: but he that **end**ureth to the **end** shall be saved. [10:23] But when t**hey** perse**cute you** in this city**, flee** ye into another**: for** verily I say unto you, Ye shall not have gone **over** the cities of Israel, till the Son of man be come. [10:24] The disciple **is not above** [his] master, n**or** the servant **above** his lord**. It is enough** for the disciple that he be as his master, and the servant as his lord**.**

If **they have called** the master of **the house** Beelze**bub, how** much more [**shall they call**] them of **his house**hold**?** [10:26] **Fear the**m not therefore: for there is nothing covered, that shall not be re**veal**ed; and hid, **that shall not be known.** [10:27] What I tell you in darkness, [that] speak ye in light: and what ye hear in the ear, [that] preach ye upon the housetops. [10:28] **And** fear not them which **kill** the body, but are not able to **kill** the soul: but

rather fear him which is able to destroy both soul and body in hell. {10:29} Are not **two sparrows** sold **for a fart**hing? and one of them shall not fall on the ground without your Father. {10:30} But **the very hairs of your head** are all numbered. {10:31} **Fear** ye not therefore, ye are of more value than **many sparrows.** [BOO!]

{10:32} Whosoever therefore shal**l confess** me before men, him will **I confess** also before my Father which is in heaven. {10:33} **But** whosoever shall deny me before men, him will **I also deny** before my Father which is in heaven. {10:34} Think not that **I am** come to send pe**ace** on earth: **I** c**am**e **not** to send peace, but a sword. {10:35} For **I** am **come to set** a man at variance against his father, and the daughter against **her moth**er, and the daughter in law **against her moth**er in law. {10:36} And a man's foes [shall be] **they** of his own household. {10:37} He that **loveth** father or **moth**er **more than me** is not worthy of me: and

48

he that loveth son or daughter more than **me is not worthy of me.**

{10:38} And he that taketh not his cross, and followeth after me, is not worthy of me. {10:39} He that **findeth** his life shall **lose it:** and he that **loseth** his life for my sake shall **find it.**

{10:40} He that **receiveth you receiveth me, and** he that **receiveth me receiveth him** that sent me. {10:41} He that receiveth a prophet in the name of a prophet shall receive a prophet's reward: **and** he that **receiveth a** righteous man in the name of a righteous man shall receive a righteous man's **reward** {10:42} And whosoever shall give **to drink** unto **one** of these **little** ones a **cup of cold** [water] only in the name of a disciple, verily I say unto you, he shall in no wise lose his reward.

{11:1} And it came to pass, when Jesus **us** had **made a** n end of commanding **ding** his twelve disciples, he departed thence to teach and to preach **in their** cities. {11:2} Now when John had heard **ear** in the prison the works of Christ, **two** [DING! DING!] of his

49

disciples. {11:3} And said unto him, Art thou he that should come, or do we look for another?

{11:4} Jesus answered and said unto them, **Go** and shew John again those things which ye do hear and **see**. {11:5} The blind receive their sight, and the lame walk, **the** lepers are **clean**sed, and the deaf h**ear, the dead are** raised up, and the **poor** have the gospel preached to them. {11:6} **And** bless**ed is [he,] whosoever** **shall not** be **offend**ed in me.

{11:7} And as they departed, Jes**us began to say** unto the multitudes concerning John, **What went** ye **out into the** **wilderness** to see? A reed shaken with **the wind?** {11:8} But **what** went ye **out for to see? A man cloth**ed in soft raiment? behold, **they** that **wear soft [clothing]** are **in** kings' **houses.** {11:9} **But what** went **ye** out for to **see?** A prophet? yea, I say unto you, and more than a prophet. {11:10} For this is [he,] of whom it is written, **Behold, I send my mess**enger before thy face, which shall prepare thy way before thee. {11:11} Verily

I say unto you. Among them that are born of women there hath not risen a greater than John the Baptist: notwithstanding he that is least in the kingdom of heaven is greater than he. {11:12} And from the days of John the Baptist until now the kingdom of heaven suffereth violence, and the violent take it by force. {11:13} For all the prophets and the law prophesied until John. {11:14} And if ye will **receive** it, this is Elias, which was for to come.

{11:15} He that hath ears to hear, let him hear. {11:16} But whereunto

shall **I liken this generation**? It is like unto **children sitting** in the markets, and calling unto their fellows, {11:17} **And saying, We have pipe**d unto you, **and ye have not danced;** we have mourned unto you, and ye have not **lame**nted. {11:18} For John came neither eating nor drinking, **and** they say, He hath **a devil**. {11:19} The Son of man **came eating** and drinking, and they say, Behold **a** man glut**ton**ous, and a winebibber, a friend of publicans and sinners. But wisdom is justified **of** her **children.**

51

[11:20] he began he to upbraid the cities wherein most of his mighty works were done, because they repented not: [11:21] Woe unto thee, Chorazin! woe unto thee, Bethsaida! for if the mighty works, which were done in you, had been done in Tyre and Sidon, they would have repented long ago in sackcloth and ashes. [11:22] But I say unto you, It shall be more tolerable for Tyre and Sidon at the day of judgment, than for you. [11:23] And thou, Capernaum, which art exalted unto heaven, shalt be brought down to hell: for if the mighty works, which have been done in thee, had been done in Sodom, it would have remained until this day. [11:24] But I say unto you, That it shall be more tolerable for the land of Sodom in the day of judgment, than for thee.

[11:25] At that time Jesus answered and said, I thank thee, O Father, Lord of heaven and earth, because thou hast hid these things from the wise and prudent, and hast revealed them unto babes. [11:26] Even so, Father: for so it seemed good in thy sight. [11:27] All things are delivered unto me of my Father: and no man knoweth the Son, but the Father; neither knoweth any man the Father, **save the** Son, and [he] to whomsoever the Son will re**veal** [him.] {11:28} Come unto me, all [ye] that labour **and a**re **heavy lad**en, and I **will give you** rest. {11:29} Take my yoke upon you, and learn of me; for I am meek and lowly in heart: and ye shall find rest unto your souls. {11:30} For my yoke [is] easy, and **my burden** is light.

{12:1} At that time Jes**us went** **on** the sab**bath day** through the corn; and his disciples were an hungred, **and began to** pluck the ears of corn, and to eat. {12:2} But when the Phari**see**s **saw** [it**,] they said unto him, Behold, thy** disciples **do that which is not lawful to do up**on **the** sab**bath day.** {12:3} **But he said un**to them, Have ye not read what David did, when he was an hungred, and they that were with him; {12:4} How he entered into the house of God, and did eat the shewbread, which was not lawful for him to eat, neither for them which were with him, but only for the priests? {12:5} Or **have ye not read** in **the law,** how that on the sabbath days the priests in the temple profane the sabbath, and are blameless**?** {12:6} But **I say unto you,** That **in**

this place is [one] greater than the temple. [12:7] But if ye had known what [this] meaneth, I will have mercy, and not sacrifice, ye would not have condemned the guiltless. [12:8] For the Son of man is Lord even of the sabbath day.

[12:9] And when he was departed thence, he went into their synagogue: [12:10] And behold, there was a man which had [his] hand withered. And they asked him, saying, Is it lawful to heal on the sabbath days? that they might accuse him. [12:11] And he said unto them, What man shall there be among you, that shall lay hold on it, and lift [it] out? a sheep, and if it fall into a pit on the sabbath day, will he not out? [12:12] How much then is a man better than a sheep? Wherefore it is lawful to do well on the sabbath days. [12:13] Then saith he to the man, Stretch forth thine hand. And he stretched [it] forth; and it was restored whole like as the other. [12:14] Then the Pharisees went out, and held a council against him, how they might destroy him. [12:15] But when Jesus knew [it,] he withdrew him**elf** from thence: and great multitudes followed him, and he healed them all; [12:16] And **charged** them that they should not make **him** known: [12:17] That it might be fulfilled which was spoken by Esaias the prophet**, saying,** [12:18] Behold my servant, whom I have chosen; **my** beloved, in whom my soul **is well** pleased: I will put my spirit upon him, and he shall **shew judgment to** the Gentiles. [12:19] He shall not strive, nor cry; neither shall **any man** hear his voice **in the streets.** [12:20] A bruised reed shall he not break, and **smoking** flax **shall** he not **quench** till he send forth **judgment** unto victory. [12:21] **And** in **his name shall** the Gentiles **trust.**

[12:22] **T**he**n was brought** unto him **one** possessed with a **devil, blind, and dumb:** and he healed him: insomuch that the blind and dumb both spake and saw. [12:23] And all the people were amazed, and said, Is not this the son of David? [12:24] But w**he**n the Phari**sees** heard [it,] they

55

This ~~fellow doth not cast out~~ **devil** , ~~but by B~~**eel**~~zebub the prince of the~~ **devils** ~~[12:25] And Jesus knew their thoughts~~, ~~and said unto them. Every kingdom divided against itself is brought to desolation: and every city or house divided against itself shall not stand: [12:26] And if Satan cast out Satan, he is divided against~~ **elf**, ~~how shall then his kingdom stand? [12:27] And if I by Beelzebub cast out~~ **devils,** ~~by whom do~~ **your children** ~~cast [them] out? therefore they~~ **shall be** ~~your judges. [12:28] But if I cast out~~ **devils** ~~by the Spirit of God~~, ~~then the kingdom of God is come unto you. [12:29] Or else how can one enter into a strong man's house, and spoil his goods, except he first bind~~ the **strong** ~~man?~~ **and** ~~then he will spoil his house. [12:30] He that is not with me is against me: and he that gathereth not with me~~ **scattereth abroad.**

~~[12:31] Wherefore I say unto you, All manner of sin and blasphemy shall be forgiven unto men: but the blasphemy [against]~~ **the**  ~~[Holy]~~ **Ghost shall** ~~not~~ **be** ~~forgiven~~ **given** ~~un~~**to men.** ~~[12:32] And whosoever speaketh a word~~

against the Son of man, it shall be forgiven him: but whosoever speaketh against the Holy Ghost, it shall not be forgiven him, neither in this world, neither in the [world] to come.

{12:33} Either make the tree good, and his fruit good; or else make the tree corrupt, and his fruit corrupt: for the tree is known by [his] fruit.

{12:34} O generation of vipers, how can ye, being evil, speak good things? for out of the abundance of the heart the mouth speaketh.

{12:35} A good man out of the good treasure of the heart bringeth forth good things: and an evil man out of the evil treasure bringeth forth evil things. {12:36} But I say unto you, That every idle word that men shall speak, they shall give account thereof in the day of judgment. {12:37} For by thy words thou shalt be justified, and by thy words thou shalt be condemned.

{12:38} Then certain of the scribes and of the Pharisees answered, saying, Master, we would see a sign from thee.

[12:39] But he answered **an**d said unto them, An **evil** and adulterous gene**rat**ion seeketh after a sign; and there **shall** no sign **be given to** it, but the sign of the prophet Jonas: [12:40] For as Jonas was three days **a**nd three nights in the **whale**'s belly; so shall the Son of man be three days and three nights in the heart of the earth**.**

[12:41] The men of Nineveh shall rise in judgment with this generation, and shall condemn it: because they repented at the preaching of Jonas; and, behold, a greater than Jonas [is] here. [12:42] The queen of **the south shall rise up** in the judgment with this generation, and shall condemn it: for she came from the uttermost parts of the earth **to hear the** wisdom of **Solo**mon; and, behold, **a great**er than **Solo**mon [is] here**.**

[12:43] When the un**clean** spirit is gone **out** of a man, he walketh through **dry places,** seeking **rest, and find**eth none. [12:44] Then he saith, I will return into **my house** from whence I came out; and when

empty, swept, and garnished **with** **an elf,** **worse than** **wicked**

While he **talked** **his** **moth** **stood without** desiring to speak with him. **Then one said unto him, Behold, thy moth** **stand without** desiring to speak with thee. **he answered and said** **, Who is my moth** **Behold my moth** **who** **shall do the will of my** **moth** .

The **out** **house** **by the sea side.**

59

that he went into a ship, and sat; **a**nd the w**hole** multitude stood **on the** shore. {13:3} And he spake many things unto them in parables, saying, Behold, a sower went forth to sow;

{13:4} **A**nd when he **sow**ed, some [seeds] fell by the way side, and the fowls came and **devoured** them up: {13:5} Some fell upon stony places, where they had not much earth: and forthwith they sprung up, because they had no deepness of earth: {13:6} And when **the sun** was up, they were **scorched**; and because they had no root, they withered away. {13:7} And **some** fell among thorns: and the thorns sprung up, and choked them: {13:8} But other fell into **good** ground, and brought forth **fruit,** some an hundredfold, some sixtyfold, some thirtyfold. {13:9} Who hath ears to hear, let him hear. {13:10} And the disciples came, and said unto him, Why speakest thou unto them in parables? {13:11} He answered **and said** unto them, Because it is given unto you to **know the mysteries of** the kingdom of heaven, but to them it is not given. {13:12} For whosoever hath, to him shall be given, and he shall have more abun**dance**: but whosoever hath not, from him shall be taken away even that he hath. {13:13} Therefore speak I to them in parables: because they seeing see not; and hearing they hear not, neither do they understand.

{13:14} And in them is fulfilled the prophecy of Esaias, which saith, By hearing ye shall hear, and

shall not under**stand**; **and see**ing ye shall see, and shall not perceive: {13:15} For t**his** people's **ear is waxed gross, and** [**their**] **ears are** dull of **hearing,** and their eyes they have closed; lest at any time **they should see** with [their] eyes, and hear with [their] ears, **and** should

understand with [**their**] **ear,** and should be converted, and I should heal them. {13:16} But blessed [are] your eyes, for they see: and **your ears**, for they **hear.** {13:17} For verily I say unto you, That **many** prophets and righteous [**men**] have **desire** to see [those things] which ye see, and have not seen [them;]

61

and to hear [those things] which ye hear, and have not heard [them.]

[13:18] Hear ye therefore the parable of the sower. [13:19] When any one heareth the word of the kingdom, and understandeth [it] not, then cometh the wicked [one,] and catcheth away that which was sown in his heart. This is he which received seed by the way side. [13:20] But he that received the seed into stony places, the same is he that heareth the word, and anon with joy receiveth it; [13:21] Yet hath he not root in himself but dureth for a while: for when tribulation or persecution ariseth because of the word, by and by he is offended. [13:22] He also that received seed

among the thorns is he that heareth the word; and the care of this world, and the deceitfulness of riches, choke the word, and he becometh unfruitful. [13:23] But he that received seed into the good ground is he that heareth the word, and understandeth [it;] which also beareth fruit, and bringeth forth, some an hundredfold, some sixty, some thirty.

{13:24} Another parable put he forth unto them, saying, **The king**dom of heaven **is** likened unto a man which sowed good seed **in his field:** {13:25} But while men slept, **his enemy** came and sowed tares among the wheat, and went his way. {13:26} But when the blade was **sprung up, and brought** forth **fruit**, then appeared the tares also. {13:27} So the servants of the householder came and said unto him, Sir, didst not thou sow good seed in thy field? from whence then hath it tares? {13:28} He said unto them, An enemy hath done this. The servants said unto him, Wilt thou then that we go and

gather them up? {13:29} But he said, Nay; lest while ye gather up the tares, ye root up also the wheat with them. {13:30} Let both grow together until the harvest: and in the time of harvest I will say to **the** r**ape**rs, **Gather** ye together first the tares, **and bind them in bundles to** burn them: but gather the wh**eat in**to **my barn.**

{13:31} Another parable put he forth unto them, saying, **The kingdom** of heaven is like to a grain of mustard seed, which a man took, and sowed

in his field: {13:32} Which indeed is the least of all seeds: but when it is grown, **is** the greatest among herbs, **a** and becometh a tree, so that the birds of the air come and lodge in the b**ranch**es thereof.

{13:33} Another parable spake he unto them; The kingdom of heaven is like unto leaven, which **a woman** took, and hid **in** three measures of meal, till the whole was leavened. {13:34} All these things **spa**ke Jesus unto the multitude in parables; and without a parable spake he not unto them: {13:35} That it might be fulfilled which was **spoke** by the prophet, **saying, I will open my mouth** in parables**; I will utter things** which have been kept secret **from the** foundation of the world. {13:36} Then Jesus sent the multitude away, and went into the **house** and his disciples came unto him, saying, Declare unto us the parable of **the tar**es of the **field** {13:37} He answered and said unto them, He that soweth the good seed is the Son of man;

{13:38} The field is the world; the good seed are the **children** of the kingdom; but the tares **are** the children of **the wicked** [one; {13:39} The enemy that sowed them is the **devil;** the harvest is **the end of the world;** and the reapers are the angels. {13:40} As therefore the tares are gathered and burned in the fire; so shall it be in **the end of this world.** {13:41} The Son of man shall send forth his angels, and they shall gather out of his kingdom all things that offend, and them which do in**iquit**y; {13:42} And shall cast them into a furnace of fire: there shall be wailing and gnashing of teeth**.** {13:43} Then shall the righteous shine forth as the sun in the kingdom of their Father. Who hath ears to hear, let him hear.

{13:44} Again, **the king**dom of heaven is like unto trea**sure hid in a field;** the which when a man hath **found, he hideth, and** for joy thereof **goeth and selleth** all that he hath**, and buyeth that field.**

{13:45} Again, **the king**dom of heaven **is** like unto **a** merchant **man, seeking** goodly **pearls:** {13:46} Who, when **he** had **found one pearl** of great price, went and sold all that he had, **and bought it.**

{13:47} Again, **the king**dom of heaven is like unto a net, that was cast into the sea, and gathered of every kind: {13:48} Which, when it was

full, they **drew** to shore, and sat down, and gathered the good into vessels, but cast the bad away. {13:49} So shall it be at the end of the world: the angels shall come forth, **a**nd sever the **wicked** from among the just. {13:50} And shall cast them into the furn**ace** of fire: there shall be wailing and gnashing of teeth.

{13:51} Jes**us saith** unto them, **Have ye understood all these things? They say** unto him, **Yea,** Lord. {13:52} **Then** said he unto them, Therefore every scribe [which is] instructed unto the kingdom of heaven is like unto a man [that is] an house**hold**er, which

66

bringeth forth out of **his** treasure [**thing**] new and old.

[13:53] And it came to pass, [that] when Jes**us** had finished these parables, he **departed** thence. [13:54] And when he was come into his own country, he taught them in their synagogue, **in**somuch that they were astonished, and said, Whence hath this [man] this wisdom, and [these] mighty works? [13:55] Is not **his** the  **car**penter's son? Is not his mother called Mary? and his brethren, James, and Joses, and Simon, and Judas? [13:56] And his sisters, are they not all with us? **When**ce **the hat**h this [**man**] all these things? [13:57] And they were **offended** in **him**. But Jesus **said** unto them, A prophet is not without honour, save in his own country, and in his own house. [13:58] And **he did not** many mighty **work**s there because of their unbelief.

[14:1] At that time **Her**od the tetrarch heard of the fame of Jesus. [14:2] And said unto his serv**ants**. This is John the Baptist; he is risen from the dead; and therefore mighty **work**s do shew **for**th the**mselves** in him.

[14:3] For Herod had laid hold on John, and bound him, and put [him] in prison for Herodias' sake, his brother Philip's wife. [14:4] For John said unto him, It is not lawful for thee to have her.

[14:5] And when he would have put him to death, he feared the multitude, because they counted him as a prophet. [14:6] But when Herod's birthday was kept, the daughter of Herodias danced before them, and pleased Herod. [14:7] Whereupon he promised with an oath to give her whatsoever she would ask. [14:8] And she, being before instructed of her mother, said, Give me here John Baptist's head in a charger. [14:9] And the king was sorry: nevertheless for the oath's sake, and them which sat with him at meat, he commanded [it] to be given [her]. [14:10] And he sent and beheaded John in the prison. [14:11] And his head was brought in a charger, and given to the damsel: and she brought [it] to her mother. [14:12] And his disciples came, and took up the body, and buried it, and went and told Jesus.

[14:13] When Jesus heard [of it,] he departed thence by ship into to a desert place apart: and when the people had heard [thereof,] they followed him on foot out of the cities. [14:14] And Jesus went forth, and saw a great multitude, and was moved with compassion toward them, and he healed their sick.

[14:15] And when it was evening, his disciples came to him, saying, This is a desert place, and the time is now past; send the multitude away, that they may go into the villages, and buy themselves victuals. [14:16] But Jesus said unto them, They need not depart; give ye them to eat. [14:17] And they say unto him, We have here but five loaves, and two fishes. [14:18] He said, Bring them hither to me. [14:19] And he commanded the multitude to sit down on the grass, and took the five loaves, and the two fishes, and looking up to heaven, he blessed, and brake, and gave the loaves to [his] disciples, and the disciples to the multitude. [14:20] And they did all eat, and were filled: and they took up of the fragments that remained twelve baskets full. [14:21] And **they** that **had eaten** were **about five thousand men, beside women and children.**

[14:22] **And straightway** Jesus constrained his disciples to **get into a ship** and **to go** before him unto **to the other side,** while he sent the multitudes **away** [14:23] **And** when he had sent the multitudes **away,** he went **up into a mountain** apart to pray: and when the evening was come, he was there alone. [14:24] **But** he ship was now in the midst of the sea, tossed with waves: for the wind **was contrary.** [14:25] And in the fourth watch of the night Jesus went un **to** them, walking on the sea [14:26] And when the disciples saw him walking on the sea, they were troubled, saying**,** It is a spirit; **and** he **cried out for fear** [14:27] But straightway Jesus spake unto them, saying, Be **of** good cheer; it is I; be not afraid. [14:28] And Peter answered him and said, Lord, if it be thou, bid me come unto thee on the **water.** [14:29] And he said, Come. And when Peter was come down out of the ship, he walked on the water, to go to Jesus. [14:30] But

70

when he saw the wind boisterous, **he was afraid; and beginning to** sink, he cried, saying, Lord, save me. {14:31} And immediately Jesus **stretch**ed forth [his] hand, and caught him, and said unto him, O thou of little faith, wherefore didst thou doubt? {14:32} And when they were come into the ship, the wind ceased. {14:33} Then they that were in **the** ship came and worshipped him, saying, Of a **truth** thou art the Son of God**.**

{14:34} And when **they were** gone over, they came **in**to **the land of** Gennesaret. {14:35} And when the men of that p**lace** had knowledge of him, they sent out into **all** that country **round about** and brought unto **him** all that were diseased**;** {14:36} And besought him that **they might** only **touch** the hem of **his garment: and** as **many** as **touched** were made **perfect**ly w**hole.**

{15:1} T**he** **came** **to** Jesus scribes and Pharisees, which were of Jeru**salem, saying,** {15:2} **Why** do thy disciples **transgress the** t**rad**ition of the **elders?** for **they wash** not **their**

71

bread. rad

God, **Honour**
thy fat **moth** : **He**
that curseth fat **moth**, let
him **eat**

his **fat**
moth **a gift**, **thou**
might **profit**;
honour **his fat** **moth** ,
be free.

he **said**
unto them,

Pharisees were offended, after they heard this saying? {15:13} But he answered and said, Every plant, which my heavenly Father hath not planted, shall be rooted up. {15:14} Let them alone: they be blind leaders of the blind. And if the blind lead the blind, both shall **fall into the ditch.** {15:15} Then answered Peter and said unto him, Declare unto us this parable. {15:16} And Jes**us said, Are ye** also yet without under**standing?** **[STAND]** {15:17} Do not ye yet under**stand** that whatsoever entereth in at the mouth goeth into the belly, and is cast out into the draught? {15:18} But those things which proceed out of the mouth come forth from the heart; and they defile the man. {15:19} **For** out of the heart proceed **evil thoughts, murders, adulteries, fornications, thefts, false witness, blasphemies:**

{15:20} These are [the things] which defile a man: but to **eat with unwashen hands** defileth not a man.

73

[15:21] Then Jesus **us went** thence, and departed into **to the coast** of Tyre and Sidon. [15:22] **And, behold, a woman** of Canaan came out of the same coasts, and cried unto him **, saying,** Have mercy on me, O Lord, [thou] Son of David; **my daughter is** grievously vexed with a devil. [15:23] But **he** answered **her** not a word. And **his** disciples came and besought **him**, saying, Send **her** away; for **she** crieth after **us.**

[15:24] But he answered and said, I am not sent but unto the lost sheep of the house of Israel. [15:25] **Then came she** and worshipped him, **saying,** Lord, **help me** [15:26] But he answered and said, It is not meet to **take the children's bread, and** to **cast** [it] **to dogs.** [15:27] **And she said,** Truth, Lord: yet the **dogs eat** of the crumbs which fall from **their masters'** table. [15:28] Then Jesus answered and said unto her, O woman, great [is] thy faith: be it unto thee even as thou wilt. And her daughter was made whole

74

from that very hour. {15:29} And Jesus departed from thence, and came nigh unto the sea of Galilee; and went up into a mountain and sat down there. {15:30} And great multitudes came unto him, having with them [those that were] lame, blind, dumb, maimed, and many others, and cast them down at Jesus' feet; and he healed them; {15:31} Insomuch that the multitude wondered, when they saw the dumb to speak, the maimed to be whole, the lame to walk, and the blind to see: and they glorified the God of Israel.

{15:32} Then Jesus called his disciples [unto him,] and said, I have because they continue with me now three days, and have nothing to eat: and I will not send them away fasting, lest they faint in the way. {15:33} And his disciples say unto him, Whence should we have so much bread in the wilderness, as to fill so great a multitude? {15:34} And Jesus saith unto them, How many loaves have ye? And they said, Seven, and a few little fishes. {15:35} And he commanded the

75

multitude to **sit down on the ground.** {15:36} And he took the seven loaves and the fishes, and gave thanks, and brake [them,] and gave to his disciples, and the disciples to the multitude. {15:37} **And they did all eat, and were filled:** and they took up of the broken [meat] that was left seven baskets full. {15:38} And **they** that **did eat** were **four thousand men, beside women and children.** {15:39} And he sent away the multitude, and took ship, and came into the coasts of Magdala.

{16:1} T**he** Pharisees **sees** also with **the Sad**ducees came, and tempting desired him that he would shew them a sign from heaven. {16:2} He answered and said unto them, When it is **evening** ye say, [It will be] fair **weather: for the sky is** red. {16:3} And in the morning, [It will be] **foul** weather to day: for the sky is red and lowring. O [ye] hypocrites, ye can discern **the face of the sky**: but can ye not [discern] the signs of the times? {16:4} A **wicked** and adulterous generation seeketh after a

sign: and there shall no sign be given unto it, but the sign of the prophet Jonas**. And he left them,**

and departed to the other side, **they had forgot** to take bread.

us said to them, Take heed and beware of **the** because we have no bread. why ye elves. have brought no bread? Do ye not yet understand ? How is it that ye do not understand bread ? beware of bread.

{16:13} When Jesus came **us came** into **to the coast** of Caesarea Philippi, he asked his disciples, **saying,** Whom do men say that I the Son of man am? {16:14} And they said, Some {say that thou art} John the Baptist: some, Elias; and others, Jeremias, or one of **the** prophets. {16:15} He saith unto them, But whom say ye that I am? {16:16} And Simon Peter **answer**ed and said, Thou art the Chr**ist**, the Son of the living God. {16:17} And Jesus answered and said unto him, Blessed art thou, Simon Barjona: for flesh and blood hath **not** revealed {it} unto thee, **but my** Father which is in heaven. {16:18} And I say also unto thee, That thou art **Pet**er, and upon this **rock** I **will build** my church: **a**nd the **gate**s of hell shall not prevail against it. {16:19} **And** I will **give** unto **thee the key**s of the kingdom of heaven: and whatsoever thou shalt bind on earth shall be bound in heaven**:** and **what**so**ever** thou shalt loose on earth shall be loosed in heaven. {16:20} Then charged he his disciples that they should tell no man he was Jesus the Christ.

[16:21] From that time forth began Jes**us** to shew unto his disciples, how that he **must go** unto Jeru**salem and** suffer many things of the elders and chief priests and scribes, and be **kill**ed, and be raised again **the third** day. [16:22] Then **Pet**er took him, and began to rebuke him, saying, Be it far from thee, Lord: this shall not be unto thee.

[16:23] But he turned, and said unto Peter, Get thee behind me, Satan: thou art an offence unto me: for thou **savour**est not **the** things that be of God, but those that be of men. [16:24] Then said Jesus unto his disciples, If any [man] will come after me, let him deny hims**elf,** and take up his cross, and follow me. [16:25] For whosoever will **save his life** shall **lose it:** and whosoever will **lose his life** for my sake shall **find it.** [16:26] For what is a man profited, if he shall gain the whole world, and lose his own soul? or what shall a man give in exchange for his soul? [16:27] For the Son of man shall come in the glory of his Father with his angels; and **the**n he shall **reward** every man according to h**is work**s. [16:28] Verily I say unto

79

you. **The**re be some stan**ding** here, which shall not taste **of death**, till they see the Son of man coming in his kingdom. **[DING!]**

[17:1] And after six days Je**us taketh** Peter, James, and John **his bro**ther, and bringeth them **up** into **a high mountain** apart. [17:2] And was transfigured before them: and his face did shine as the sun, and his raiment was white as the light. [17:3] **And, behold,** there **a** **pear**ed unto them, Moses and Elias **talking** with him. [17:4] Then answered Peter, and said unto Jesus, Lord, it is good for us to be here: if thou wilt, let us make here three tabernacles; one for thee, and one for Moses, and one for Elias. [17:5] While he yet spake, behold, a bright cloud overshadowed them: and behold a voice out of the cloud**, which said, This is my** be**love**d Son, in whom **I am well** p**leased;** hear ye him. [17:6] And when the disciples heard [it,] **they fell on their face, and were sore** afraid. [17:7] And Jesus came and t**ouch**ed them, and said, Arise, and be not afraid. [17:8] And when they had lifted up their eyes, they saw no man, save Jesus only. [17:9] And as **they**

RESTORE:
- sanity
- equality
- compassion
- respect
- humility

came down from the mountain, Jesus charged them, saying, Tell the vision to no man, until the Son of man be risen again from the dead. [17:10] And his disciples asked him, saying, Why then say the scribes that Elias **must** first **come**? [17:11] **And** Jesus answered and said unto them, Elias truly shall first come, and **restore all things** [17:12] But I say unto you, That Elias is come **already,** and **they knew** him not, but have done unto him whatsoever **the list**ed. Likewise shall also the Son of man suffer of them. [17:13] Then the disciples understood that he spake unto them of John the Baptist.

[17:14] And when they were come to the multitude, there came to him a [certain] man, kneeling down to him, and saying, [17:15] Lord, have mercy on **my son** for he **is lunatic**, **and** sore **vexed:** for oftimes **he falleth into the fire** and oft into the **water.** [17:16] And I brought him to thy disciples, and they could not cure him. [17:17] Then Jesus answered and said, **O** faithless and **perverse generation,** how

81

long shall I be with you? **how long shall I suffer you?** Bring him hither to me. {17:18} And Jesus rebuked the devil; and he departed out of him: and the child was cured from that very **hour.** {17:19} Then came the disciples to Jesus apart, and **said, Why** could **not** we cast him out**?** {17:20} And Jesus said unto them, **Because** of your unbelief: for verily I say unto **you** If ye **have** faith as a grain of mustard seed, ye shall say unto **to** this mountain, **Remove** hence to yonder place**lace;** **and** it shall **remove;** and nothing shall be impossible unto you. {17:21} Howbe**it** this kind goeth not out but by prayer and **fast**ing. {17:22} And while they abode in Galilee, Jesus said unto them, The Son of man shall be betrayed into the hands of men: {17:23} **And** they shall **kill him**, and the third day he shall be raised again. And they were exceeding sorry**.**

{17:24} And when **the**y were come to C**ape**rnaum, they that **received** tribute [**money**] came to Peter**, and said,** Doth not your master pay tribute? {17:25} He saith, Yes. And when he was come into the house, Jesus

82

prevented him, saying, **What thinkest thou** Simon? of whom do the kings of the earth take custom or tribute? of their **own children, or** **strangers?** [17:26] Peter saith unto him, Of **strangers.** Jesus saith unto him, Then **are the** **children free.** [17:27] Notwithstanding, lest we should offend them, go thou to the sea, and cast an hook, and **take** up **the** fish that first co**meth** up: and when thou hast opened his mouth, thou shalt find a piece of **money:** that **take, and give** un**to** them for **me** and thee.

[18:1] At the same time came the disciples unto Jesus saying, Who is the gre**ate**st in the kingdom of heaven? [18:2] And Jesus called **a** **little** child unto him, and set him in the midst of them. [18:3] And said, Verily I say unto you,

Except ye be converted, and become as **little** children, ye shall not enter into the kingdom of heaven. [18:4] Whosoever therefore shall humble him**elf** as this little child, **he** same is gre**ate**st in the kingdom of heaven. [18:5] And whoso shall receive **one** such **little** **child** in my name receiveth me. [18:6] But whoso shall offend **one of these little ones**

which believe in me, it **were better for him** that a millstone were hanged about his neck, and [that] he were drowned in the depth of the sea.

[18:7] Woe unto **the world** because of offences! for it must **needs** be that **offences** come; but woe to that man by whom **the offence cometh!** [18:8] Wherefore **if thy hand or thy foot offend thee,** cut them off, and cast [them] from thee: **it is better for** thee to enter into life halt or maimed, rather than having two hands or two feet to be cast into everlasting fire. [18:9] **And if thine eye offend thee,** pluck it out, and cast [it] from thee: **it is better** for thee to enter into life with one eye, rather **than having two eyes** to be cast into hell fire. [18:10] Take heed that ye despise not one of these little ones; for I say unto you, That in heaven their angels do always behold the face of my Father which is in heaven. [18:11] For the Son of man is come to save that which was lost.

[18:12] **How think ye?** if a man have **a hundred sheep,** and one of them be gone astray, doth he **not** leave the **ninety and nine,** and goeth

84

into the mountains, and seeketh that which is gone astray**?** {18:13} And if so be that he find it, verily I say unto you, he **rejoice**th **more** of that [**sheep,**] than of the **ninety and nine** which went not astray**.** {18:14} Even so it is not the will of your Father which is in heaven, that one of **these little ones should perish.** [HOORAY!]

{18:15} **More**over, if thy brother shall tre**spas**s against thee**,** go and tell him his fault between thee and him alone: if he shall hear thee, thou hast gained thy brother. {18:16} But if he will not hear [thee, then] take with thee **one or two more,** that in the mouth of two or **three** witnesses every word may be established**.**

{18:17} And if **he shall neglect** to hear **them**, tell [it] unto the church: but if he neglect to hear the church, let him be unto thee as an he**at**hen man and **a pub**lican**.**

{18:18} Verily I say unto you, **What**so**ever** ye **shall bind** on earth **shall be bound** in heaven: and whatsoever ye shall loose on earth shall be

85

loosed in heaven. {18:19} Again I say unto you, **if two of you** **agree** on earth as touching any thing that they shall ask, it shall be done for them of my Father which is in heaven. {18:20} For where two or three are gathered together in my name, there am I in the midst of them. **[Agreed]**

{18:21} **The**n came **Pet**er to him, and **said,** Lord, how oft shall my **bro**ther sin against me, and I forgive him? Till **seven times?** {18:22} Jesus

saith unto him, I say **no**t unto thee, Until seven times: but, Until **seventy times seven.**

{18:23} Therefore is **the king**dom of heaven likened unto a certain king, which would take account of his servants. {18:24} And when he had begun to reckon, one was brought unto him, which **owed him ten thousand** talents. {18:25} But forasmuch as he had not to pay, his lord commanded him to be sold, and his wife, and **children**, and all that he had, and payment to be

made. {18:26} The servant **he**refore fell down, and wor**shipped him**, saying, Lord, have patience with me, and I will pay thee all. {18:27} Then the lord of that servant was moved with compassion, and loosed him, and forgave him the debt. {18:28} But the same servant went out, and found **one** of his fellow servants, which owed him an **hundred** pence: and he laid **hands** on him, **and took** [**him**] **by the throat, saying,** Pay me that thou owest. {18:29} And his fellowservant fell down at his feet, and besought him, saying, **Have patience** with me, and **I will pay thee** all. {18:30} And he would not: but went and cast him into prison, till he should pay the debt. {18:31} So w**he**n his fellowservants saw what **was** done, they were **very sorry**. [**Sorry**] and came and told unto their lord all that was done. {18:32} **Then** his lord, after that **he** had **called him**, said unto him, O thou **wicked** servant, I forgave thee all that debt, because thou desiredst me: {18:33} Shouldest not thou also have had comp**ass**ion on thy fellowservant, even as I had pity on thee? {18:34} And his lord was w**rot**h, and delivered him to the tormentors, till **he** should pay all that was due un to him. [18:35] So likewise shall my heavenly Father do also unto you, if ye from your hearts forgive not every one his brother their tresp ass .

[19:1] And it came to pass, [that] when Jes us had finished these sayings, he departed from Galilee, and came in to the coast of Judaea beyond Jordan; [19:2] And gr eat multitudes followed him; and he healed them there. [Delicious!]

[19:3] T he Phari sees also came unto him, tempting him, and saying unto him, Is it lawful for a man to put away his wife for every cause? [19:4] And he answered and said unto them, Have ye not read, that he which made [them] at the beginning made them male and female,

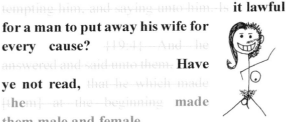

[19:5] And said, For this cause shall a man leave fat her and moth er, and shall leave to his wife: and they twain shall be one flesh? [19:6] Wherefore they are no more twain, but one flesh. What therefore God hath joined together, let not man put a under . [19:7] They say unto him,

88

Why did Moses then command to give a writing of divorcement, and to put her away? [19:8] He saith unto them, Moses because of the hardness of **your** h**ear**ts suffered you to put away your wive**s**: but from the **begin**ning it was not so. [19:9] And I say unto you, Whosoever shall put away his wife, except [it be]  for **fornication**, **and** shall marry another, committeth **adultery**: and whoso marrieth her which is put away doth commit adultery.

[19:10] His disciples say unto him, If the case of the man be so with [his] wife, it is not good to marry. [19:11] But he said unto them, All [men] cannot receive this saying, save [they] to whom it is given. [19:12] For **there are some eunuchs, which were** so **born from** [**their**] **mother's womb: and there are some eunuchs, which were made eunuchs of men: and there be eunuchs, which have made the**ms**elves eunuchs for the king**dom of heaven's sake. He that is able to receive [it,] let him receive [it.]

[19:13] Then were he brought unto him little children, that he should put [his] hands on them, and pray: and the disciples rebuked them. [19:14] But Jesus said, Suffer little children, and forbid them not, to come unto me: for of such is the kingdom of heaven. [19:15] And he laid his hands on them, and departed thence.

[19:16] And, behold, one came and said unto him, Good Master, what good thing shall I do, that I may have eternal life? [19:17] And he said unto him, Why callest thou me good? [there is] none good but one, [that is,] God: but if thou wilt enter into life, keep the commandments. [19:18] He saith unto him, Which? Jesus said, Thou shalt do no murder, Thou shalt not commit adultery, Thou shalt not steal, Thou shalt not bear false witness, [19:19] Honour thy father and [thy] mother: and, Thou shalt love thy neighbor as thy elf.

[19:20] The young man saith unto him, All these things have I kept from my youth up: what lack I yet? [19:21] Jesus said unto him, If thou wilt be perfect, go [and] sell that thou hast, and give to the poor, and thou shalt have treasure in

[19:23] **Then said** Jesus **us** unto his disciples, Verily I say unto you, That **a rich man shall** hardly enter into the kingdom of heaven. [19:24] And again I say unto you, It is easier for a camel to go through the eye of a needle, than for a rich man to **enter** into the kingdom of God. [19:25] When **his** disciples h**ear**d [it,] they were exceedingly a**maze**d, **saying,** Who then can be saved? [19:26] But Jesus beheld [them,] and said unto them, With men **this is impossible**: but with God all things are possible.

[19:27] **The**n answered **Pet**er and said unto him, Behold, we have forsaken all, and followed thee; what shall we have therefore? [19:28] And Jesus said unto them, Verily I say unto you, That ye which have followed me, in the regeneration when the Son of man **shall sit in the** throne of his glory, ye also shall sit upon twelve thrones, judging the twelve tribes of Israel. [19:29] And every one that hath forsaken **house**, or brethren, or sisters,

91

or father, or mother, or wife, or children, or lands, for my name's sake, shall receive an hundredfold, and shall inherit everlasting life. [19:30] But many [that are] first shall be last; and the last [shall be] first.

[20:1] For the kingdom of heaven is like unto a man [that is] an householder, which went out early in the morning to hire labourers in his vineyard. [20:2] And when he had agreed with the labourers for a penny a day, he sent them into his vineyard. [20:3] And he went out about the third hour, and saw others standing idle in the

marketplace, [20:4] And said unto them; Go ye also into the vineyard, and whatsoever is right I will give you. And they went their way. [20:5] Again he went out about the sixth and ninth hour, and did likewise. [20:6] And about the eleventh hour he went out, and found others standing idle, and saith unto them, Why stand ye here all the day idle? [20:7] They say unto him, Because no man hath hired us. He saith unto them, Go ye also into the vineyard: and whatsoever is right, [that] shall ye receive. [20:8] So when even was come, the lord of the vineyard saith unto his steward. Call the labourers, and give them [their] hire, beginning from the last unto the first. {20:9}

one lousy cent

And when they came that [were hired] about the eleventh hour, they received every man a penny. {20:10} But when the first came, they supposed that they should have received more; and they likewise received every man a penny. {20:11} And when they had received it, they murmured against the goodman of the house. {20:12} Saying, These last have wrought [but] one hour, and thou hast made them equal unto us, which have borne the burden and heat of the day. {20:13} But he answered one of them, and said, Friend, I do thee no wrong: didst not thou agree with me for a penny? {20:14} Take [that] thine [is,] and go thy way: I will give unto this last even as unto thee. {20:15} Is it not lawful for me to do what I will with mine own? Is thine eye evil, because I am good? {20:16} So the last shall be first, and the first last: for many be called, but few chosen.

{20:17} And Jesus going up to Jerusalem took the twelve disciples apart in the way, and said unto them, {20:18} Behold, we go up to

salem

to **eat** **him**

Then came **the moth** **children**, **desiring a certain thing of him.** **he said**, **What**?

Are ye able to drink **I shall**

drink

They say, **We are able.** **Ye** **all drink**

[DRINK] **, and**

sit on my right hand, and on my left. is not mine to give, but [it shall be given to them] for whom it is prepared of my Father.

{20:24} And when the ten heard [it,] they were moved with indignation against the two brethren. {20:25} But Jes**us** called them [unto  him,] and **said,** Ye know that the princes of the Gentiles **exercise** dominion over **them, and** they that are gr**eat** exercise authority upon **them.** {20:26} But **it shall** not **be so** among you: but whosoever will be **great** among you, let him be your minister; {20:27} And whosoever will be chief among you, **let** him be your servant: {20:28} Even as the Son of man came not to be ministered unto, but to minister, and to give his life a ransom for many. {20:29} And as **the**y departed from Je**rich**o, a gr**eat** multitude followed **him.**

{20:30} And, behold, **two blind men** sitting by the way side, when they heard that Jesus passed by, **cried out, saying,** Have **mercy** on us, O Lord, [thou] Son of David. {20:31} And the multitude rebuked them, because **they should**

hold their peace: but they cried the more, saying, Have mercy on us, O Lord, [thou] Son of David. {20:32} And Jesus stood still, and called them, and said, What will ye that I shall do unto you? {20:33} They say unto him, Lord, that our eyes may be opened. {20:34} So Jesus had comp**ass**ion [on them,] **and touch**ed **their eyes** and **immediately** their eyes received sight, and they followed him.

{21:1} And when they drew nigh unto Jer**us**alem, and were **come to** Bethphage, unto the **mount** of Olives, then sent Jesus two disciples, {21:2} Saying unto them, Go into the village over against you, and straightway ye shall find **an ass** tied, and a colt with her: loose [them,] and bring [them] unto me. {21:3} And if any [man] say ought unto you, ye shall say, The Lord hath need of them; and straightway he will send them. {21:4} All this was done, that it might be fulfilled which was spoken by the prophet, saying, {21:5} Tell **ye** the **daughter** of Sion, Behold, thy King come**th unto thee, meek, and

sitting upon an ass, and a colt the foal of an ass. {21:6} And the disciples went, and did as Jesus commanded them. {21:7} And brought the ass, and the colt, and put on them their clothes, and they set [him] thereon. {21:8} And a very great multitude spread their garments in the way; others cut down branches from the trees, and strawed [them] in the

HELLO MY NAME IS US!

way. {21:9} And the multitudes that went before, and that followed, cried, saying, Hosanna to the Son of David: Blessed [is] he that cometh in the name of the Lord; Hosanna in the highest. {21:10} And when he was come into Jerusalem, all the city was moved, saying, Who is this? {21:11} And the multitude said, This is Jesus the prophet of Nazareth of Galilee.

{21:12} And Jesus went into the temple of God, and cast out all them that sold and bought in the temple, and overthrew the tables of the moneychangers, and the seats of them that sold doves,

97

{21:13} And said unto them, It is written, My house shall be called the house of prayer; but ye have made it a den of thieves.

{21:14} And **the blind** and the lame came to him in the temple; and he healed them. {21:15} And when the chief priests and scribes **saw the** wonderful things that he did, and the **children** **crying** in the temple, and saying, Hosanna to the Son of David; **they were so** displeased **{21:16}** And said unto him, Hearest thou what these say? And Jesus saith unto them, Yea; have ye never read, Out of the mouth of babes and sucklings thou hast perfected praise?

{21:17} And **he left** them, and went out of the city into Bethany; **and** he lodged there. {21:18} Now in the morning as he **returned** into the city, he hungered. {21:19} And when **he saw a fig tree** in the way, he came to it, and found nothing thereon, but leaves only, **and said** unto it, Let **no fruit** grow on thee hence for**war**d for **ever**. And presently the fig tree withered away. {21:20} And when the disciples saw [it,] they marvelled, saying, How soon is **the fig tree** withered away!

answered and said,

whatever.

the
temp  was teaching
what author? who gave
this author to them

?

the elves say,

fear people; for they

them. Neither tell I you by what authority I **do** these **things.**

[21:28] But what **a thin**k ye? A [certain] **man** had two sons: and he came to the first, and **said,** Son, **go** work **to** day in **my** vineyard. [21:29] He answered and said, I will not: but afterward he repented, and went. [21:30] And he came to the second, and said likewise. And he answered and said, I [go,] sir: and went not. [21:31] Whether of them twain did the will of [his] father? They

say unto him, The first. Jesus saith unto them, Verily I say unto you, That the **pub**licans and the harlots go into the kingdom of God be**for**e you. [21:32] For John came unto you in **the** way of **righteous**ness, and ye believed him not: but the publicans and the **harlots** believed him: and ye, when ye had seen [it,] repented not afterward, that ye might **believe him.**

[21:33] **Hear** another parable: There was a certain householder, which planted a vineyard, and hedged it round about, and digged a winepress in it, and built a tower, **a**nd let it out

to hus**band**men, and went into **a** far **country**: {21:34} And when the time of the fruit drew near, he sent his servants to the hus**band**men, that **they might** receive the fruits of it. {21:35} And the husbandmen took his servants, and **be**at one, and killed another, and **stoned** another. {21:36} Again, he sent o**the** **servants** more than the first: and they did unto them **like**wise. {21:37} But last of all he sent unto **them** his son, saying, **They** will **revere**nce my son. {21:38} But when **the** hus**band**men saw the son, **they said among the** s**elves,** This is the heir; **come, let us** kill him, and let us **seize** on his inheritance. {21:39} And they caught him, and cast [him] out of the vineyard, and slew [him.] {21:40} When the lord therefore of **the** vineyard co**meth,** what will he do unto those husbandmen? {21:41} They say unto him, He will miserably destroy those wicked men, and will let out [his] vineyard unto other husbandmen, which shall render him the fruits in their seasons.

{21:42} Jesus saith unto them, Did ye never read in the scriptures, The stone which the builders rejected, the same is become the head of the corner: this is the Lord's doing, and it is marvellous in our eyes? {21:43} Therefore say I unto you, The kingdom of God shall be taken from you, and given to a nation bringing forth the fruits thereof. {21:44} And whosoever shall fall on this stone shall be broken: but on whomsoever it shall fall, it will grind him to powder. {21:45} And when the chief priests and Pharisees had heard his parables, they perceived that he spake of them. {21:46} But when they sought to lay hands on him, they feared the multitude, because they took him for a prophet.

{22:1} And Jesus answered and spake unto them again by parables, and said, {22:2} The kingdom of heaven is like unto a certain king, which made a marriage for his son, {22:3} And sent forth his servants to call them that were bidden to the wedding: and they would not come. {22:4} Again, he sent forth other servants, saying, Tell them which are bidden, Behold, I have prepared my dinner: my oxen and [my]

~~fat~~l~~ings [are]~~ **killed**. ~~and~~ **all** ~~things [are] ready: come unto the marriage. {22:5} But they made light~~ **of** ~~[it,] and went their ways, one to~~

his farm. ~~another to his merchandise: {22:6} And the remnant took his~~ **servants, and** ~~entreat~~**ate** ~~[them]~~ **spitefully,** ~~and slew [them.] {22:7} But when the king heard [thereof,] he was wroth: and he sent forth his armies, and destroyed those murderers, and burned up their city. {22:8} Then saith he to his servants, The wedding is ready, but~~ **they** ~~which~~

were ~~bidden were not worthy. {22:9} Go ye therefore into the~~ **high**~~ways, and as many as ye shall find, bid to the marriage.~~ **.** ~~{22:10} So those servants went out into the~~

~~highways,~~ **and** ~~gathered together al~~l ~~as many as they~~ **found**, ~~both bad and good: and~~ **the** **wedding** ~~was f~~**urn**~~ished with guests.~~

~~{22:11} And when~~ **the king** ~~came in to see the guests, he~~ **saw** ~~there~~ **a** ~~man which had not on a wedding~~ **garment:** ~~{22:12} And he saith unto him, Friend, how camest thou in hither not having~~ **a** ~~wedding~~ **garment?** ~~And~~ **he was**

103

speechless [22:13] Then said the king to the servants, Bind him hand and foot, and take him away, and cast [him] into outer darkness; there shall be weeping and gnashing of teeth. [22:14] For many are called, but few [are] chosen.

[22:15] Then went the Pharisees, and took counsel how they might entangle him in [his] talk. [22:16] And they sent out unto him their disciples with the Herodians, saying, Master, we know that thou art true, and teachest chest the way of God in truth, neither carest thou for any [man:] for thou regardest not the person of men. [22:17] Tell us therefore, What thinkest thou? Is it lawful to give tribute unto Caesar, or not? [22:18] But Jesus perceived their wickedness, and said, Why tempt ye me, [ye] hypocrites? [22:19] Shew me the tribute money. And they brought unto him a penny. [22:20] And he saith unto them, Whose [is] this image and superscription? [22:21] They say unto him, Caesar's. Then saith he unto them, Render therefore unto Caesar the things which are Caesar's: and unto God the things that are God's. {22:22} When they had heard [these words,] they marvelled, and left him, and went their way.

{22:23} The same day came to him the **Sad**ducees, which say that there is no resurrection, and asked him, {22:24} Saying, Master,  Moses said, If a **man** die, **having** no **children,** his brother **shall** marry his wife, and **raise** up seed unto his brother. {22:25} Now there were with us **seven** brethren**:** and **the first,** when he had married a wife, deceased, and, having no issue, left his wife unto his brother: {22:26} Likewise **the second also, and the third, unto the seventh.** {22:27} And last of all the woman died also. {22:28} Therefore in the resurrection whose wife shall she be of the **seven?** for they all had her. {22:29} Jesus answered and said unto them, Ye do err, not knowing the scriptures, nor the power of God. {22:30} For in the resurrection they neither marry, nor are given in marriage, but are as the angels of God in heaven. {22:31} But as touching the resurrection of the

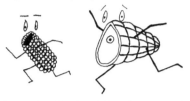

he had put the **Sad** **lawyer asked** him a question, **saying,** {22:36} Master, which [is] the gr**eat** commandment **men** in the law**?** {22:37} Je**us said** unto him, Thou shalt love the Lord thy God with all thy heart, and with all thy soul, and with all thy mind. {22:38} This is the first and gr**eat** commandment. {22:39} And the second [is] like unto it, Thou shalt love **thy neighbour as thy** elf. {22:40} On these two

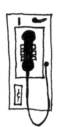

us **asked them,** What **he** said **, Sit on my right hand, till I make thin footstool : then call him , how is he ? ask him more questions.**

observe, observe and do; but do not say, and do not. For heavy be a hem on men's shoulders;

107

the elves will move
hem with one
finger . they

enlarge the
garments, And

go in the
markets .

call your

greatest

elf shall and he shall
hum . [HUMMMMMM]

you
see hypocrites! shut up
your elves, the

scribes and Pharisees, **hypocrites**! for ye devour
widows' houses, and for a
pretence make long prayer:
therefore ye **shall** receive the
gr**eat**er **damnation**. {23:15}
Woe unto **you**, scribes and
Pharisees, **see hypocrites**! for ye
comp**ass** sea and **land** to make
one proselyte, and when he is made, ye make
him **two**fold more the **child** of hell than
yours**elves**. {23:16} Woe unto **you**, [ye] blind
guides, which say, Whosoever **shall wear** by
the temple, it is **nothing; but** whosoever shall
s**wear** by the **gold** of the temple, he is a debtor!
{23:17} [Ye] fools **and** blind: for whether is
gr**eat**er, the **gold**, or the temple that sanctifieth
the gold? {23**:**18} And, Whosoever shall s**wear**
by the altar, it is **nothing**; but whosoever
sweareth by the gift that is upon it, he is guilty.
{23:19} [Ye] **fools** and blind: for whether [is]
gr**eat**er, the gift, or the al**tar** that sanctifieth the
gift? {23**:**20} Whoso therefore shall s**wear** by
the al**tar, wear**eth by it, and by all **things**
thereon. {23:21} And whoso shall swear by the
temple, sweareth by it, and by him that dwelleth
therein. {23:22} And he that shall swear by
heaven, sweareth by the throne of God**, and** by

him that sit~~teth~~ here. ~~{23:23} Woe unto you,~~ ~~scribes and Pharisees,~~ ~~hypocrites! for ye pay tithe~~ ~~of mint and anise and~~ ~~cummin, and have omitted the weightier~~ ~~[matters] of the law, judgment,~~ mercy, ~~and faith:~~ ~~these ought~~ ye ~~to~~ have ~~done, and not~~ to ~~leave the~~ ~~other undone. {23:24} [Ye] blind guides, which~~ ~~strain at a gnat, and~~ swallow a camel.

~~{23:25} Woe unto you, scribes and Pharisees,~~ ~~hypocrites! for ye~~ ~~make~~ clean the ~~outside of the~~ cup and ~~of the~~ platter, ~~but within~~ the~~y are full of extortion and excess.~~ ~~{23:26} [Thou]~~ blind ~~Pharisee,~~ see within the cup and platter, ~~that~~ the outside ~~of them~~ may be clean also.

~~{23:27} Woe unto you, scribes and Pharisees,~~ ~~hypocrites! for~~ ye ~~are like unto whited~~ ~~sepulchres, which indeed~~ ~~app~~ear be~~autiful~~ ~~outward, but are within~~ full of dead ~~[men's]~~ bones, ~~and of all unclean~~ness. ~~{23:28} Even so~~

 &

110

ye also outwardly appear righteous unto men, but within ye are full of hypocrisy and iniquity.

{23:29} Woe unto you, scribes and Pharisees, hypocrites! because ye build the tombs of the prophets, and garnish the sepulchres of the righteous. {23:30} And say, If we had been in the days of our fathers, we would not have been partakers with them in the blood of the prophets. {23:31} Wherefore ye be witnesses unto your elves that ye are the children of them which killed the prophets.

{23:32} Fill ye up then the measure of your fathers. {23:33} [Ye] serpents, [ye] generation of vipers, how can ye escape the damnation of hell?

{23:34} Wherefore, behold, I send unto you prophets, and wise men, and scribes: and [some] of them ye shall kill and crucify; and [some] of them shall ye scourge in your synagogues, and persecute [them] from city to city: {23:35} That upon you may come all the righteous blood shed upon the earth, from the blood of righteous Abel

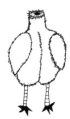

unto the blood of Zacharias son of Barachias, whom ye slew between the temple and the altar.

[23:36] Verily I say unto you, All these things shall come upon this generation. [23:37] O Jerusalem, Jerusalem, [thou] that killest the prophets, and stonest them which are sent unto thee, **how often would I** have **gather**ed thy **children** together, even as a hen **gather**eth her **chicken**s under [her] **wings, and hold your** house is left unto you **late** desolate. [23:39] For I say unto you, Ye shall not see me **hen**ceforth, till ye sh**all** say, Blessed [is] he **that** co**meth** in the name of the Lord.

[24:1] And Jes**us** went out, and **departed** from the temple: **and** his disciples **came** to [him] for **to shew** him

t**he build**ings of the temple. [24:2] And Jesus said unto them, See ye not all these **things**? Verily I say unto you, **There shall** not **be** left here one stone upon another, that sh**a**ll not be **thrown down.**

112

[24:3] And as he sat upon the mount of Olives, the disciples came unto him privately, saying, Tell us, **when shall** these things **be**? and what [shall be] the sign of thy coming, and of **the end of the world?** [24:4] And Jes**us answered and said** unto them, Take heed that no man deceive you. [24:5] For **many** shall come in my name, saying, I am Christ; and shall deceive **many** [24:6] And ye shall hear of wars and **rum**ours of **wars**. see

that ye be not troubled: for all [these things] **must come to pass,** but **the end is not yet.** [24:7] For nation shall rise against nation, and kingdom against kingdom: and **there shall be** famines, **a**nd **pest**ilences, and earthquakes. **in** divers **places.** [24:8] All these [are] the beginning of sorrows.

[24:9] **The**n shall they de**liver** you up to be afflicted, and **shall kill you:** and ye shall be **hate**d of **all** nations for my name's sake. [24:10] And then shall many be **offend**ed, **and** shall **betray one another, and** shall **hate one another.**

{24:11} And many false prophets shall rise, and shall deceive many. {24:12} And because iniquity shall abound, **the love of** many sh**all wax** cold. {24:13} But he that **shall endure unto the end**, the same shall be saved. {24:14} And this gospel of the kingdom shall be preached in all the world for a witness unto all nations; and then shall the end come.

{24:15} When ye therefore shall see the abomination of desolation, spoken of by Daniel the prophet, **stand in the** holy p**lace,** (whoso readeth, let him under**stand**:) {24:16} Then let them which be **in** Judaea flee into the mountains: {24:17} Let him which is on the housetop not come down to take any thing out of his house: {24:18} Neither let him which is in the field return back to take **his clothes** {24:19} **And** woe unto them that are with child, and to them that give **suck** in those days! {24:20} But pray ye that your **flight** be not in the winter, neither **on** the sab**bath day:**

{24:21} For then shall be great tribulation, such as was not since the beginning of **the world** to this time, no, nor ever **shall be** {24:22} **And** except those days **should be shortened,** there should no flesh be saved: but for the elect's sake those days **shall be shortened.** {24:23} Then if any man shall say unto you, Lo, here [is] Christ, or there; believe [it] not.

{24:24} For there shall arise false Christs, and false prophets, and shall shew great signs **an**d wonders; insomuch that, if [it were] possible, they shall deceive the very elect. {24:25} Beh**old, I have t**old you** before. {24:26} Wherefore if they **shall say unto you,** Behold, [he is] in the desert: go not forth: **behold,** he is in **the secret chamber**s: believe [it] not. {24:27} **For** as the lightning co**meth** out of the east, and shineth even unto the west; so shall also the coming of the Son of man be**.**

{24:28} For wheresoever the carcase is, there will the eagles be gathered together. {24:29} Immediately after the tribulation of those days shall the sun be darkened, and **the moon** shall not give her light, and the s**tar**s **shall fall** from heaven, **and the pow**ers of the heavens **shall** be **shake**n. [24:30] And then shall appear the sign of the Son of man in heaven: and then shall all the tribes of **the earth** mourn, and they shall see the Son of man coming in the clouds of heaven with **pow**er and great glory.

[24:31] And he shall send his angels with a gr**eat** sound of **a** trum**pet**, and they shall gather together his elect from the four winds, **from one end** of heaven **to the other**. [24:32] Now learn a parable of the fig tree; When his branch is yet tender, **, and** putteth forth **leave**s, ye know that summer is nigh: [24:33] So likewise ye, when ye sh**all** see all these **things**, know that it is **near**, [even] at **the door** . [24:34] Verily **I say unto you, This** gene**rat**ion **shall not pass**, till all these things be fulfilled. [24:35] Heaven and earth shall pass away, but **my** words shall not p**ass** away.

[24:36] But of that day and hour k**no**weth **no** [man,] **no, no**t the angels of heaven, but my , but my Father only. [24:37] But as the days of **No**e

116

[were,] so shall also the coming of the Son of man be.

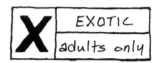

[24:38] For as in the days that were before the flood they **we eat**ing **and drink**ing, marrying and giving in marriage, **until** the day that Noe entered into the ark, [24:39] And knew not until the flood came, and took them all away; so shall also the coming of the Son of man be. [24:40] Then shall two be in the field; the one shall be taken, and the other left. [24:41] **Two** [**women shall be**] **grinding at the mill;** the one shall be taken, and **the other** left.

[24:42] **Watch** therefore: for ye **know** not **what hour your** Lord doth come. [24:43] But know this, that if the goodman of the house had known in what **watch** the **thief would** come, he would **have watch**ed, **and** would **not** have suffered his house to **be broken** up. [24:44] Therefore be ye **also**

117

ready for in such **an hour** as ye think **not** the Son of man **meth.**

{24:45} Who then is a faithful and wise servant, **who**m his **a**th **mad**e **ruler over his** household, to give them **meat** in due season**?** {24:46} Blessed [is] **that** servant, whom his lord when he **meth shall** find so doing. {24:47} Verily I say unto you, That he shall **make him ruler over all** his goods**.** {24:48} But and if that evil servant shall say in his heart, My lord delayeth his coming; {24:49} And shall begin to **smite** [his] fellowservants**, and** to **eat** and drink with the drunken; {24:50} The lord of that servant shall come in a day when he looketh not for [**him,**] and **in an hour** that he is not aware of, {24:51} And shall cut him asunder, and appoint [him] his portion with the hypocrites: there shall be weeping and gnashing of teeth**.**

{25:1} Then shall the kingdom of heaven be likened unto **ten virgins**, which took their lamps, and went forth to meet the bridegroom. {25:2} And five of them were wise, and five

[were] foolish. {25:3} They that [were] foolish took their lamps, and took no oil with them: {25:4} But the wise took oil in their vessels with their lamps. {25:5} While the bridegroom tarried, they all **slumbered and slept** {25:6} **And** at midnight there was a cry **made**. Behold, the bridegroom co**meth**: go ye out to meet him. {25:7} **Then all those virgins** arose, and trimmed their lamps. {25:8} And the foolish **said** unto the wise**,** Give us of your **oil**, for our lamps are gone out. {25:9} But the wise answered, saying, [Not so;] lest there be not enough for us and you: but go ye rather to them that sell, and buy for **your elves.** {25:10} And

while they went to buy, the bridegroom came: and they that were ready went in with him to the marriage: and the door was shut. {25:11} Afterward came **also the** other **virgins**, saying, Lord, Lord, open to us. {25:12} But he answered and **said,** Verily I say unto you, **I know you** not. {25**:**13} **[WHISPER] Watch** therefore, for ye know neither the day nor the hour wherein **the** Son of man co**meth.**

119

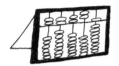

{25:14} For the king dom of heaven is as a man travelling into to a far count ry, [who] called his own servants, and delivered unto them his goods. {25:15} And unto one he gave five talents, to another two, and to another one; to every man according to his several ability; and straightway took his journey. {25:16} Then he that had receive d the five talents went and traded with the same, and made [them] other five talents. {25:17} And likewise he that [had] receive d two, he also gain ed other two. {25:18} But he that had receive d one went and digged in the earth, and hid his lord's money. {25:19} After a long time the lord of those servants cometh, and reckoneth with them. {25:20} And so he that had received five talents came and brought other five talents, saying, Lord, thou deliver edst unto me five talents: behold, I have gained beside them five talents more. {25:21} His lord said unto him, Well done, [thou] good and faithful servant: thou hast been faithful over a few things, I will make thee ruler over many things; enter thou into the joy of thy lord. {25:22} He also that had receive d two talents came and

said, Lord, thou **deliver**edst unto me **two** talents: behold, I have **gain**ed **two** other talents **beside** them. {25:23} His lord said unto him. **Well done, good and faithful** servant; thou hast been faithful over a few things, I will make thee ruler over many things: enter thou into the joy of thy lord. {25:24} Then he which had received the one talent came and said, Lord, I knew thee that thou art an hard man, reaping where thou hast not sown, and gathering where thou hast not strawed:

{25:25} And I was afraid, and went and hid thy talent in the earth: lo, [there] thou hast that is] thine. {25:26} His lord answered and said unto him, [Thou] wicked and slothful servant, thou knewes t that I reap where I sowed not, and **gather** where I have not st**raw**ed: {25:27} Thou oughtest therefore to have put my money to the exchangers, and [then] at my coming I should have received mine own with usury. {25:28} Take therefore the **talent** from him, and give [it] un**to** him which hath ten talents. {25:29} For unto every one that hath shall be given, and he

121

shall have abun**dance**, but from him that hath not shall be taken **away** even that which he hath. {25:30} And cast ye **the unprofitable** servant into outer **darkness**: there shall be weeping and gnashing of teeth.

{25:31} When the Son of man shall come in his glory, and all the holy angels with him, then shall he sit upon the throne of his glory: {25:32} And before him shall be gathered all nations: and **he** shall separ**ate** them one from ano**ther**, as a shepherd divideth [his] **sheep** from the goats: {25:33} And he shall set the sheep on his right h**and**, but the **goats** on the left. {25:34} **Then** shall the **he** King **say** unto them on his right hand**,** Come, ye blessed of my Father, inherit the kingdom **prepare**d for you from the foundation of **the world**: {25:35} **For** I was an hung**red**, and ye gave me **meat**: I was thirsty**, and** ye gave me **drink**: I was a stranger, and ye took me in: {25:36} **Naked**, and ye clothed me: I was sick, and ye visited me: I was in prison, and ye came unto me**.** {25:37} Then shall **the right**eous **answer** him, saying, Lord, when saw we thee an hungred, and fed [thee]**?** or thirsty, and gave

122

[thee] **drink**? {25:38}
When saw we thee a
stranger, and took
[thee] in? or **naked,**
and clothed [thee?]
{25:39} Or when saw

we thee sick, or in prison, and came unto thee?
{25:40} And the King shall answer and say unto
them, Verily I say unto you, Inasmuch as ye have
done [it] unto one of the least of these my
brethren, ye have done [it] unto me. {25:41}
Then shall he say also unto them on the left
hand, **and** Depart from me, ye cursed, into
everlasting fire, **prepared**
for **the** devil **evil** and his angels:
{25:42} For I was an
hungred **red** and ye gave me no
meat: I was thirsty, and ye
gave me no **drink** {25:13} I
was a stranger, and ye took

me not in: **naked,** and ye clothed me not: sick,
and in prison, and ye visited me not. {25:44}
Then shall they also answer him, saying, Lord,
when **saw** we **thee** an **hung**red, or athirst, or a
stranger, or **naked,** or sick, or in prison, **and** did
not minister unto thee? {25:45} Then shall he
answer them, saying, Verily I say unto you,

123

To what purpose [is] this waste? {26:9} For **this ointment might** have been sold for much, and **give** to the poor. {26:10} When Jesus understood [it,] he said unto them, Why trouble ye the woman? for she hath wrought a good work upon me. {26:11} For ye have **the poor** always with you; but me ye have not **always** {26:12} For in that she hath **pour**ed **this ointment** on my body, she did [it] for my burial. {26:13} Verily I say unto you, **Wheresoever** this gospel shall be preached **in the** w**hole** world, [there] shall also this, that this woman hath done, be told for a memorial of her. {26:14} Then one of the twelve, called Judas Iscariot, went unto the chief priests, {26:15}

And said [unto them,] What will ye **give me**, **a**nd I will de**liver** him unto you? And they **coven**anted with him for thirty pieces of **silver**. {26:16} And from that time he sought opportunity to be**tray** him. {26:17} Now the first [day] of the [feast of] unleavened bread the disciples came to Jesus, saying unto him, **Where wilt thou** that we prepare for thee to **eat the** p**ass**over? {26:18} And he said, Go into the city to such a man, and say unto him, The Master saith, My time is at hand; I will **keep the** p**ass**over **at thy house** with my disciples. {26:19} And the disciples did as Je**us** had ap**pointed** them; **and** they made ready **the** p**ass**over. {26:20} Now when the even was come, he **sat down** with the twelve. {26:21} **And** as **he did eat** he said,

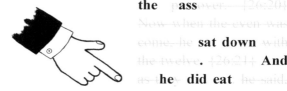

Verily I say unto you, that one of you shall betray me. {26:22} And they were exceeding sorrowful, and began every one of them to say unto him, Lord, is **it** I? {26:23} **And he** answered and **said,** He that **dip**peth **his hand** with me **in the dish**, the same shall be**tray** me. {26:24} The Son of man goeth as it is written of him: but woe unto that man by whom the Son of man is betrayed! it had been **good for** that man if he had not been born. {26:25} Then Judas, which betrayed **him,** answered and said, Master, is it I? He said unto him, Thou hast said.

{26:26} And as they were **eat**ing, Jesus took b**read, and** blessed [it,] and b**rake** [it,] and gave

[it] to the disciples**, and** said, Take, **eat**; this is my body. {26:27} And he took the **up,** and gave thanks, and gave [it] to them, saying, **Drink** ye **all of it;** {26:28} For this is my blood of the new testament, which is shed for many for the remission of sins. {26:29} But I say unto you, I will not **drink** henceforth of this fruit of the vine, until that **a** day when I **drink** it new **with** you in my **her** Father's kingdom. {26:30} And when they had sung an hymn, they went out into the mount of **Olives.**

{26:31} Then saith Jes **us** unto them, All ye shall be off**ended** beca**use of** me **his** night: for it is writ**ten**, I will smite the shepherd, and the **sheep** of the flock shall be scattered **abroad.**

{26:32} But after I am risen again, I will go before you into Galilee. {26:33} Peter answered and said unto him, Though **all** [**men**] **shall** be **offend**ed because of thee, [**yet**] will I **never** be **offend**ed. {26:34} Jesus said unto him, Verily I say unto thee, **That** this **is** night, **before** the cock crow, **thou** shalt **deny me** th**rice.**

127

{26:35} **Peter** said unto him, Though I **should die** with thee, yet will I not deny thee. Likewise **also** said all the disciples.

{26:36} **Then** cometh Je **us** with them unto a place called Gethsemane, and saith unto the disciples, Sit ye here, while I **go** and pray **yonder**. {26:37} And he **to**ok with him Peter and **the** two sons of Zebedee, and began to be sorrowful and **very heavy** {26:38} Then saith he unto them, My soul is exceeding sorrowful, even unto death: **tar**ry ye here, and watch with me. {26:39} **And** he went **a little fart**her, and **fell on** his **face,** and prayed, **saying,** O my Father, if it be possible, **let this** cup **pass** from me:  **never**theless not as I will, but as thou **wilt.** {26:40} And he cometh unto the disciples, and findeth them asleep, and saith unto Peter, What, **could ye not watch** with **me one hour?** {26:41} **Watch** and pray, that ye enter not into temptation: the spirit indeed [is] willing, but the flesh **[is] weak.** {26:42} He went away again the second time, and prayed, saying, O my Father, if

this cup may not pass away from me, except I drink **it**, thy will be done. {26:43} And he came and **found them asleep** again: for their eyes were heavy. {26:44} And he left them, and went away again, and prayed the third time**, saying the** same **words**. {26:45} Then cometh he to his disciples, and saith unto them**, Sleep on now, and** take [your] rest **behold, the hour is** at **hand, and** the Son of man is be**tray**ed into the hands of sinners. {26:46} Rise, let us be going**: behold, he is** at **hand** that doth be**tray me.**

{26:47} And while he yet spake, lo, Judas, **one of the** twelve, came, and with him a great multitude with swords and staves, from the

chief priests and elders of the **people**. {26:48} Now he that betrayed him gave them a sign, saying, Whomsoever **I shall kiss**, that same is he: hold him fast. {26:49} **And** forthwith he came to Jes**us**, and **said,** Hail, master; and **kiss**ed him. {26:50} And Jesus said unto him, **Friend,** wherefore art thou come? Then came they, and laid hands on Jesus, and took him.

{26:51} And, behold, one of them which were with Jes**us stretched out** |**his**| **hand,** and drew his sword, **and struck** a servant of the high priest's, and smote **off his** ear. {26:52} Then said Jesus unto him, Put up again thy sword into his p**lace:** for all they that take the sword shall perish with the sword. {26:53} Thinkest thou

that I **can**not now pray to my Father, and he shall presently **give** me **more** than twelve **leg**ions of angels? {26:54} But how then shall the scriptures be fulfilled, that thus it must be? {26:55} In that same hour said Jesus to the multitudes, Are ye come out a**s against a thief with words** and staves for to take me? I sat daily with you teaching in the temple, and ye laid no hold on me. {26:56} But all this was done, that the scriptures of the prophets might be fulfilled. Then all the disciples forsook him, and **fled.**

{26:57} And they that had laid hold on Jes**us led** |him| away to Caiaphas the high priest, where the scribes and the elders were assembled. {26:58} But Peter followed him afar off unto **the** high priest's palace, and went in, **and sat** with the servants, **to see the end.** {26:59} Now the chief priests, and elders, and all the council, sought false witness against Jesus, to put him to death; {26:60} But found none: yea, though many false witnesses came, [yet] found they none. At t**he** last came two false witnesses, {26:61} And **said,** This [fellow] said, **I am able to destroy** the temple of God, and to build it in three days. {26:62} And the high priest arose, and said unto him, Answerest thou **nothing? what** [is it which] these witness against thee**?** {26:63} But Jesus held his peace. And the high priest answered and said unto him, I adjure thee by the living God, that thou tell us whether thou be the Christ, the Son of God. {26:64} Jesus saith unto him, Thou hast said: nevertheless I say unto you, Hereafter shall ye see the Son of man sitting on the right hand of power, and coming in the clouds of heaven. {26:65} Then the high priest rent his clothes, saying, He hath spoken blasphemy; what further need have we of

witnesses? behold, now ye have heard his blasphemy.

{26:66} **What think ye? They answered and said,** He is **guilty** of death. {26:67} Then did **he spit in his** face, and **buffet**ed him: and others  smote [him] with the palms of their hands. {26:68} Saying, Prophesy unto us, thou Christ, Who is he that smote thee?

{26:69} **Now** Peter sat without in **the** palace: and a **damsel** came unto him, saying, Thou also wast with Jesus of Galilee. {26:70} But he **denied** before [them] all, saying, I know not what thou sayest. {26:71} And when he was gone out into the porch, another [maid] saw **him, and said** unto them that were there**, This [fellow] was** also with Jesus of Nazareth. {26:72} And again he **denied** with an oath, I do not know the man. {26:73} And after a while came unto [him] they that stood by, and said to Peter, Surely thou also art [one] of them; for thy speech bewrayeth thee. {26:74} **he began to curse and** to **swear, [saying,]** I know not the

132

man. And immediately the **cock** crew. {26:75} **And** Peter **remember**ed **he** word of Jesus, which **said** unto him. Before the **cock** crow, thou

shalt deny me **thrice.** [Cock! Cock! Cock!] **And he went out** and wept **bitterly.** {27:1} When the morning was come, all the chief priests and elders of the people took counsel against Jes**us** to **put him to death:** {27:2} And when they had bound him, **the**y led [him] away, and delivered him to Pontius Pil**ate the governor.**

{27:3} **The**n Judas, which had betrayeth him, when he saw that he was condemned, repented hims**elf,** and **brought** again the **thirty pieces of silver** to the chief priests and elders. {27:4} Saying, I have sinned in that I have betrayed the innocent blood**.** And they said, What [is that] to us? See thou [to that.] {27:5} **And** he cast down **the** pieces of silver in the temple, and departed, and went and hanged hims**elf.** {27:6} And the chief priests **took the silver pieces** and said, It is not lawful for to put them into the treasury, because it is the price of blood. {27:7} And they took counsel, **and bought** with them **the** pot er's **field, to bury strangers in.** [27:8] Wherefore **that field was** called, The field of blood, unto this day. [27:9] Then was ful**filled** that which was spoken by Jeremy the prophet, saying, **And he took the** thirty pieces of silver, the price of him that was valued, whom they of the **children** of Israel did value; [27:10] **And** gave them for **the pot**ter's **field**, as the Lord appointed me**. [Right on!]**

[27:11] And Jes**us stood** before the governor: **and** the governor asked him, saying, Art thou the King of the Jews? And Jesus said unto him, Thou sayest. [27:12] And when he was accused of the chief priests and elders, he answered nothing. [27:13] Then said Pil**ate** unto him, Hearest thou not how **many** things they witness against thee? [27:14] And he answered him to never a word; insomuch that the governor marvelled greatly. [27:15] Now at [that] feast the governor was wont to release unto the **people** a pris**on**er, whom they would. [27:16] And they had then **a** no**table** prisoner, called Barabbas. [27:17] Therefore when they were gathered

134

together, Pilate said unto them, Whom will ye that **at** I release **a** unto you? **Bar**abbas, or Jesus which is called Christ? {27:18} **:** For he knew that for **envy** they had de**liver**ed him.

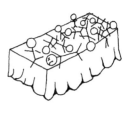

{27:19} When **he** was set down on the judgment seat **eat his wife** sent unto him, saying, Have thou nothing to do with th**at** just man: for I have suffered many things this day in a dream because of him. {27:20} But the chief priests and elders persuaded the multitude **that** they should ask **Bar**abbas, and destroy Jesus. {27:21} The governor answered and said unto them, Whether of the twain will ye that **I** release unto you? They said, Barabbas. {27:22} Pil**ate** saith unto **them**. What sh**all** I do then with Jesus which is called Christ? [They] all say unto him, Let him be crucified. {27:23} And the governor said, **Why**, what **evil** hath he done**?** But they cried out the more, saying, Let him be crucified. {27:24} When Pilate saw that he could prevail nothing, but [that] rather a tumult was

ALL YOU CAN EAT

made, he took water, and washed [his] hands
before the multitude, saying, I am innocent of
the blood of this just person: see ye [to it.
[27:25] Then answered all the people, and said,
His blood [be] on us, and on **our children.**

[27:26] Then **release**d he Barabbas unto **the**m:
and when he had scourged Jesus, he delivered
[him] to be crucified. [27:27] Then the **soldiers**
of the governor took Jesus into the common hall,
and gathered unto him **the** whole band [of
soldiers. [27:28] And they st**ripped** him, and
put on him a scarlet **robe.** [27:29] And when
they had platted a crown of thorns, they put [it]
upon his head, and a reed in his right hand: and
they bowed the knee before him, and mocked
him, saying, Hail, King of the Jews! [27:30]
And they spit upon him, and
took the reed, and smote him
on the head. [27:31] And
after that they had mocked
him, they took **the robe** off
from him, and put his own
raiment on him, and led him

away to crucify [him. [27:32] And as they
came out, **they found** a man of Cyrene, Simon **on**
by name: him **the**y compelled to **bear** his cross:

{27:33} And when **they** were come unto a place called Golgotha, that is to say, a place of a **skull.**

{27:34} They gave him vinegar to drink mingled with gall: and when he had tasted [thereof,] he would not drink. {27:35} And **he** crucified him, and **parted his garments,** casting lots: that it might be fulfilled which was spoken by the prophet, They parted my garments **among them,** and upon **my vest**ure did they cast lots**.** {27:36} And **sit**ting

down they watched him there: {27:37} And set up over his head his accusation written, THIS IS JESUS THE KING OF THE JEWS. {27:38} Then were there two thieves crucified with him, one **on the right hand, and** another **on the left.**

{27:39} **And** they **that** p**ass**ed by reviled him, wagging their **head**s, {27:40} And saying, Thou that dest**roy**est **the temp**le, and buildest [it] in three days, save thyself. If thou be the Son of God, come down from the cross. {27:41} Likewise also the chief priests mocking [him,] with the scribes and elders, **said,** {27:42} He saved **the**rs; hims**elf** he **cannot save**. If he be the King of Israel, let him now come down from **the** cross, and we will believe him. [27:43] He **trusted** in God; let him deliver him now, if he will have him: for he said, I am the Son of God.

[27:44] The thieves also, which were crucified with him, cast the same in his teeth.

[27:45] Now from the sixth hour there was darkness over all the land unto the ninth hour. [27:46] And about the ninth hour Jesus cried with a loud voice, saying, Eli, Eli, lama sabachthani? that is to say, My God, my **Go**d, why hast thou forsaken me? [27:47] Some of them that stood there, when they heard [that,] said, This [man] **call**eth **for** Elias. [27:48] And straightway one of them ran, and took **a spunge,**

and **fill**ed [**it**] with vinegar, **and** put [it] on a reed, and gave him to drink. [27:49] The **rest** said, Let be, let us see whether Elias will come to save him.

138

[27:50] Jes**us**, when he **had** cried again with **a loud** voice, yielded up the ghost. [27:51] And, behold, the veil of the temple was rent in twain from the top to the **bottom;** and the earth did quake, and the rocks rent;

[27:52] And **the** g**raves were open**ed**; and many bodies** of the saints which slept arose, [27:53] And **came out of the** g**raves after** his resurrection, and went into the holy city, and appeared unto many. [27:54] Now when the centurion, and they that were with him, watching Jesus, saw **the earthquake, and** those things that were done, **they feared greatly**, saying, Truly this was the Son of God. [27:55] **And many women were** there be**holding** afar off, which followed Jesus from Galilee, **mini**stering unto him: [27:56] Among which was Mary Magdalene, and Mary the **moth**er of Zebedee's **children.**

[27:57] When the even was come, there came **a** rich **man of** Ari**math**aea**, named Jose**ph**,** who also himself was Jesus' disciple: [27:58] He went to Pil**ate** **an**d b**egg**ed the body of Jesus**.

139

$\pi = 3.1415$
926535897932
384626433832
$7950288...$

Then Pilate commanded **a** the body to be delivered. {27:59} And **Jose** had taken the body, he wrapped it in a clean linen cloth. {27:60} And laid it in his own new tomb, which he had hewn out in the **rock**: **and** he **rolled** a great stone to the door of the sepulchre, and departed. {27:61} And there was Mary Magdalene, and the other Mary, sitting over against the sepulchre.

{27:62} Now the next day, that followed the day of the preparation, the chief priests and Pharisees came together unto Pilate. {27:63} Saying, Sir, we remember that that deceiver said, while he was yet alive, After three days I will rise again. {27:64} Command therefore that the sepulcher be made sure until the third day, lest his disciples come by night, and steal him away, and say unto the people, He is risen from **the dead:** so **the last** error **shall be worse than the first**.

{27:65} Pilate said unto them, Ye have a watch: **go** your way, **make** [it] as sure as ye can.

{27:66} So they went, and made the sepulchre sure, sealing the stone, **and set**ting **a watch.**

{28:1} In **the end** of the sabbath, as it **began** to dawn **toward the first** [**day**] **of the week,** came Mary Mag**dale**ne and the other Mary to see the sepulchre. {28:2} And, behold, there was a great earthquake: for the angel of the Lord descended from heaven, and **came and rolled** back the st**one** from the door, **and sat upon** it.

{28:3} **His** countenance was like **lightning,** and his raiment white as snow: {28:4} **And** for fear of him **he** keepers **did shake, and became** as **dead** [men.] {28:5} And the angel answered and said unto **the women, Fear not** ye: for I know that ye seek Jesus, which was crucified.

{28:6} He is not here: for he is risen, as he said. **Come, see the** pl**ace** where the Lord lay. {28:7} **And go quickly,** and tell his disciples that he is risen from **the dead**: and, behold, he goeth before you into Galilee: there shall ye **see** him: lo, I have told **you.** {28:8} And they departed

141

quickly from the sepulchre with fear and great
joy; and did run to bring his disciples **word.**

[28:9] And as they went to tell his disciples,
behold, Jes**us** met them, saying, All hail. And
they came and **held him by the feet** and
worshipped him. [28:10] T**hen said** Jesus unto
them**, Be** not **afraid**: go tell my brethren that
they go into Galilee, and there shall they see me.
[28:11] Now when they were **go**ing, be**hold**,
some of **the watch** came into the city, and
shewed unto the chief priests all the things that
were done. [28:12] And when they were
assembled with the elders,
and had **take**n counsel, **the**
gave large **money** unto the
soldiers, [28:13] Saying,
Say ye, His disciples came
by night, and stole him [away] while we slept**.**
[28:14] And if this come to the governor's ears,
we will persuade him, and **secure** you. [28:15]
So they took **the money**, and did as they were
taught: and this saying is commonly reported
am**on**g the Jews until **this day.**

[28:16] **Then** the eleven disciples went away
into Galilee, into a mountain where Jes**us** had
ap**pointed** them. [28:17] And when they saw
him, they worshipped him: but some doubted.
[28:18] And Jesus came and spake unto them**,**

saying, All power is given unto me in heaven and in earth. {28:19} Go ye therefore, and teach all nations, baptizing them **i**n the n**am**e of the Father, and of the Son, **a**nd of the Holy **Ghost:** {28:20} Teaching them to observe all things whatsoever I have commanded you: and, lo, **I am** with you always, [even] unto **the end of the world.** Amen.

The End

146

Fun Quiz

Mark an inverted X in the space in front of the correct answer(s). Personally, I recommend using a yellow, No. 2 pencil. **No! Cheating!**

1. Eve was tempted by a ____ in the garden of Eden?
    __ a) Snake
    __ b) Bear
    __ c) Serpent
    __ d) Chippendales dancer

    c (non-descript serpent)

2. Eve took a bite out of _____ from the tree of life in the garden of Eden.
    __ a) a pear
    __ b) an apple
    __ c) a watermelon
    __ d) Who the hell knows? The *Bible* doesn't say what it was. It could've been a banana. That would've added an extra layer to her temptation. And it was the tree of knowledge, not life.
    __ e) an apple. And it was the tree of knowledge, not life.

    p

3. Which book(s) of the *Bible* did Jesus
   write?
   __ a) Proclamations
   __ b) the Gospel of Jesus
   __ c) Revelation
   __ d) The Last Temptation of Christ
   __ e) He didn't write a single word. But
   he did draw something in the dirt one
   time. But the *Bible* doesn't say what it
   was.

   e (John 8:6-8)

4. Jesus:
   __ a) was homeless.
   __ b) was unemployed.
   __ c) mooched food from strangers.
   __ d) hung out with criminals.
   __ e) was a refugee seeking asylum in
   Egypt after receiving a death threat.*

   *All the above (*Matt. 2:13-15)*

5. Noah's ark (a really, really, big boat)
   was large enough to hold approximately
   6.5 million +/- land dwelling species, x2
   (male/female) = 13,000,000 creatures?
   __ a) True
   __ b) False
   __ c) Why drown all the remaining
   animals? What did they do wrong? Why

not just have humans spontaneously combust? That would be a more believable story, and fun to watch!

Probably b (c is also acceptable)

6. *The Ark Encounter*, a theme-park built around a "life-size" replica of Noah's ark, which claims that dinosaurs were also onboard, filed a lawsuit in 2019 against their insurance company for flood damage.

    __ a) True
    __ b) False
    __ c) Please be true! Please be true!
    __ d) LOLLLLLLL!!!!!

    a (c and d are also acceptable.)

7. The *Bible* contained 80 books until 1885, when fourteen books were removed from the word of God by most protestant denominations. Today, most *Bibles* only contain how many books?

    __ a) 80
    __ b) 14
    __ c) 0
    __ d) 66

    80 − 14 + 0 = 66

8. The following verses are in the *Bible*?

   Matthew {28:16} Ye all waste not your hard-earned riches on thy homeless, thou sick, ye poor. Let the little children figureth things out for themselves, it builds character. Ye wealth shall ye protect, for it is ye wealth that protecteth you. {28:17} Burn thy clothing when ye tire of wearing them. Giveth not to those who can't affordeth them. Is it thy fault they are lazy and poor? Thou hungry and needy should stop being so greedy. By consolidating all the wealth into ye own pocket, only then shall ye obtain peace.

   __ a) Probably not. But it would explain a lot of things if they were.
   __ b) Yes?
   __ c) Maybe?
   __ d) No?
   __ e) Whichever one prevents me from burning in hell!

   a, d, or e

150

9. In Luke 6:5-9, Jesus was attending the Olympics in Greece when he commanded all athletes to give him full credit every event they win. And if they even dare think about blaming him for losing, they will be playing all future events on a burning lake of fire.

___ True

___ False

___ Half True

___ Half False

___ a) It wasn't the Olympics. It was a regional track and field tournament.

___ b) He never said that. But I do want to shove my boot up every athlete's ass when they say, "It's was all Jesus out there today. He obviously loves me and wants my opponents to rot in hell! Now let's go party!"

___ c) It's not in Luke. It's Matthew 8:7

___ d) Sports weren't invented until the mid-1400's CE.

b (False is also acceptable.)

151

152

Jesus Said WHAT?!

Since self-righteous hypocrites love to quote the *Bible* to attack their perceived enemies, I made a condensed list of Jesus' quotes they should reference before they scream in public.

Whatever the source, most of the core messages attributed to him are noble guidelines for living a better life and being a decent, contributing member of society. But you should not have to burn in hell for failing to adhere to them all. "A" for effort!

And yes, curiously enough, these rules for entering the gates of heaven do resemble a *socialist* agenda. Call it what you will, but according to the *Bible*, Jesus said the following:

Wealth:

- Sell your possessions and give to the poor.
- Give in secret and not where others can see you giving.
- A rich man shall not enter the gates of heaven.
- You cannot serve both God and money.
- Any one of you who does not renounce all that he has cannot be my disciple.

153

Socialism:

- The righteous care about justice for the poor, but the wicked have no such concern.
- Help the needy.
- Heal the sick.
- Feed the hungry.
- Give drink to the thirsty.
- Shelter the homeless.
- Protect the children.
- Comfort the imprisoned.

Don't be a dickhole:

- Be sincere, not a hypocrite.
- Judge not or be judged.
- He who is without sin cast the first stone.
- Love your neighbor as yourself.
- Do unto others as you would have them do unto you.
- Do good to those that hate you.
- Forgive those who wrong you.
- Love your enemies.
- Blessed are the peace makers.
- All who draw the sword will die by the sword.
- We are all equal in the eyes of the Lord.
- God loves everyone.

References

- Monty Python's *The Life of Brian*
- XTC – *Dear God*
- *The Bible* – King James Version
- 2,664 +/- church services
- 50+ years of suffering through Christian hypocrisy

Under the Influence

- Kurt Vonnegut
- Gary Larson
- George Carlin
- Bourbon
- Joseph Campbell
- Bill Hicks
- Chip Kidd
- The Beatles
- Rick and Morty
- Archer
- The Simpsons
- Futurama
- Looney Tunes

Petition to Boycott Begat

Warren Hicks	in your head (Hello!)
Carrie Alter	Fun House
AMANDA & JEFF	SAME HOUSE NOW
Heather Gordon	Henry's fort
Amy & Peter	Glass House
Susan Harbage Page	The one with the view
Rachel Herrick	Warren's nightmares
IANA HOCHBAUM	3 doors down
Harriet Hoover	Traveling Circus
Kelly & Brad	Van by the river
Stacey Kirby	The Bureau
Bryce Lankard	the 9th circle
Kelly & GEORGE	OVERLOOK, ROOM 237
Alysa	Witness protection
JESSICA & ANDREW	DON'T TAP THE GLASS!
Stacy Bloom Rexrode	33 Hell or Highwater Ln
LAURA RITCHIE	GREEN HOUSE
LIEN, NIKO & MARK	RIGHT TURN ON RED
Sydney Steen	over yonder
MARTHA THORN	DOG HOUSE
Justin Tornow	Virgo
Chris Vitiello	foxhole
Tim Walter	Fruit Loops